Pocket
History

Pocket History

ANITA GANERI
HAZEL MARY MARTELL
BRIAN WILLIAMS

Philip Steele • Keith Lye

p

This edition published in 2000
This is a Parragon Book

Parragon
Queen Street House
4 Queen Street
Bath BA1 1HE, UK

2 4 6 8 1 0 9 7 5 3 1

Produced by Miles Kelly Publishing Ltd
Unit 11, Bardfield Centre, Great Bardfield, Essex, CM7 4SL

British Library Cataloguing-in-Publication Data
A catalogue record for this book is available from the
British Library.

Editor: Clive Gifford
Design: Angela Ashton
Project Manager: Sarah Eason
Production Assistant: Ian Paulyn
Editorial Assistant: Helen Parker

ISBN 0-75253-465-3

Colour reproduction DPI Colour Limited
Printed in Italy

CONTENTS

DISCOVERING
THE PAST

What is history? In its broadest sense, history is the story of people – the study of our past. Some historians look at important events, such as wars and governments, while others examine the lives of ordinary people. Our world today is shaped by decisions and actions made decades, centuries or even thousands of years ago. By understanding the past we may be able to gain a more balanced view of the present.

◁ A cuneiform writing tablet. Cuneiform was the first system of writing and the oldest tablets date from about 5500 years ago. Ancient written records like this are extremely valuable. Before writing was invented, history was passed on by word of mouth.

The basic aims of history are to record and explain our past. Historians study a range of written and oral (spoken) evidence. Combined with archaeology (the study of the things people have left behind them, such as buildings and objects), historians interpret the facts to build up a picture of previous times.

The first people to study history seriously were the ancient Greeks. In the 5th century BC, the Greek historian Herodotus (called the Father of History) set out to write an accurate record of the wars between the Greeks and the Persians to preserve the details of the time. The study of archaeology is a much more recent

◁ A miniature painting from the Duc de Berry's Très Riches Heures. Pictures like this tell us a great deal about life in medieval Europe, such as the clothes people wore, the jobs they did and the food they ate.

development; only beginning in a scientific way in the 18th century.

Interpreting the evidence is a fascinating part of a historian's or archaeologist's job. It is important to note that all accounts of history are people's interpretations of events at the time. Exaggeration, fading memory, not having all the facts and bias (being influenced by a certain point of view) can influence the account. Historians also have to be careful that their own views and attitudes don't influence their interpretation of historic texts.

History is not just concerned with the long distant past. History is the story of our lives – what is news today will be history tomorrow. Change can be sudden and dramatic, with ideas and systems thought to be fixed quickly overturned.

△ This carved ivory mask was worn as an ornament by the oba, or king, of Benin. Benin was a powerful empire in West Africa that was at its height between the 14th and 17th centuries.

◁ △ Navigational instruments like these were used in the 15th century by explorers in search of new lands. Inventions like these reveal the type of technology people used in the past.

7

HISTORICAL EVIDENCE

Historians look for evidence by researching a wide range of documents and records called historical sources. Primary sources are accounts written by people involved in the events, and include wills, maps, letters and diaries.

◁ *Julius Caesar (c. 101–44 BC) was a great general who wrote an account of his conquest of Gaul (France). History is sometimes written by those who take a major part in it.*

Historians look for evidence about people's beliefs from prayer books and religious documents and also rely on birth, death and marriage registers and population surveys called censuses. Historians also search through secondary sources – studies of primary sources made at a later date, such as newspaper reports.

Texts are not always written on paper. Over the centuries, people have written on clay, bone, silk, metal, stone and wood. Some cultures which never developed writing have kept records in other ways. For example the advanced

Inca civilisation used knotted lengths of string, called quipus, to record information.

Oral history, passed on down by word of mouth from generation to generation, is an important source of information. Such evidence often tells of migrations, exploration and great battles. Historians, today, record oral evidence onto tape and film.

◁ *The letters of the Viking alphabet, called runes, were carved on wood, metal and stone. Some rune stones tell stories from Viking history recalling battles and heroic deeds.*

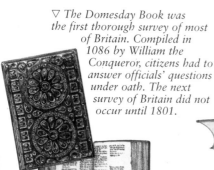

▽ *The Domesday Book was the first thorough survey of most of Britain. Compiled in 1086 by William the Conqueror, citizens had to answer officials' questions under oath. The next survey of Britain did not occur until 1801.*

▽ *Leonardo da Vinci (1452–1519) was a pioneer inventor and artist. This reconstruction of his flying machine was taken from detailed designs he made.*

ARCHAEOLOGICAL EVIDENCE

Archaeology is the study of the physical remains of the past using scientific methods to analyse finds and build a picture of the past. Archaeologists study objects (artefacts), features (buildings) and ecofacts (seeds, animal and human bones). Artefacts such as pottery, glass and metal survive well, although they are often broken into many fragments. Objects made of organic materials, such as wood, leather and fabric, rarely survive – they quickly rot away.

◁ *This is the body of a woman buried in Denmark in AD 95. The peat bog she was found in has preserved her remains.*

When archaeologists discover a site they want to examine, they set up an excavation, or dig. They carefully remove layers of earth, recording even the smallest evidence of past human activity. The specific date of an object may be found by examining historical records or by comparing it with other similar finds whose date is known. There are also scientific techniques, such as radiocarbon dating which can be used to date objects between about 40,000 years ago and AD 1500.

▽ *This wall painting is from the Lascaux Caves in France. It was painted by prehistoric hunters in about 15,000 BC.*

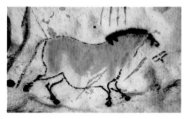

▽ *Stonehenge, in England, was built between about 2800 and 1100 BC. No one is exactly sure what it was used for, but it may have been an astronomical observatory or a giant calendar.*

THE ANCIENT WORLD

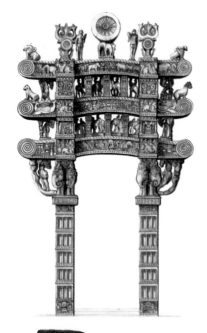

The period from 4 million years ago to AD 500 is known as the Ancient World. During this time, incredible changes occurred. This period stretches from the arrival of the first human beings, some 2.5 million years ago, to the fall of the Roman Empire around AD 500.

Our earliest ancestors are believed to have first appeared in Africa, having evolved from man-apes who left the trees and discovered how to walk upright. Over thousands of years, they learned how to hunt, how to make tools and how to make and use fire for warmth and for cooking food.

Throughout the world, early people lived by hunting animals and gathering wild fruit, roots and nuts to eat. Then, about 10,000 years ago, an extraordinary change took place. People learned how to grow their own crops and raise their own animals for food. For the first time in history, people began to build permanent homes, followed by towns and cities.

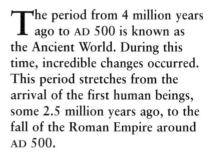

By about 5000 BC, the world's first civilizations began to emerge along the banks of rivers where the land was extremely rich for farming. The Sumerians, Assyrians and Babylonians built magnificent cities on the fertile plains between the Tigris and Euphrates rivers. The ancient Egyptians flourished along the river Nile. By about 500 BC, important civilizations had also appeared in India, China, Persia and in North and South America.

The mighty civilizations of Greece, then Rome, appeared and played major roles in shaping the modern world. From Greece came discoveries in politics, philosophy and science. These were spread farther afield by the Greek conquerer, Alexander the Great, and by the Romans, who were great admirers of the Greeks. The Romans added many achievements of their own and, by the 1st century AD, they ruled over the most powerful empire ever seen. By AD 500, the Roman Empire had fallen and the period, known as the Middle Ages had begun.

THE FIRST HUMANS

L ife on our planet began some 3,200 million years ago, with tiny cells that lived in the sea. The first human-like creatures did not appear until man-apes came down from the trees they lived in and began to walk on two legs.

The most complete man-ape (Australopithecus) skeleton was found in Ethiopia, East Africa, in 1974. Nicknamed 'Lucy' by the archaeologists who discovered her, she stood just over a metre tall, about as tall as a 10-year-old girl. When she died, 3 million years ago, she was 40 years old.

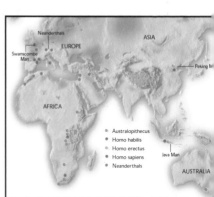

△ *This map shows where important fossil remains of early people have been discovered.*

*Australopithecus
(Southern ape)
4–1.5 million
years ago – Africa*

*Homo habilis
(Handy man)
2.5–1.5 million
years ago – Africa*

*Homo erectus
(Upright man)
1.5 million–
200,000 years ago –
Africa, Asia, Europe*

*Homo sapiens
neanderthalensis
(Neanderthal man)
120,000–30,000
years ago – Africa,
Asia, Europe*

▷ *The Great Hall of the Bulls provides a dramatic entrance to the Lascaux Caves. The walls are covered with painted and engraved animals moving in herds or files.*

As man-apes evolved into early people, they gradually became less and less like apes. They developed larger brains and bodies designed for walking upright, with longer legs than arms – the reverse of apes. Standing upright left their hands free for holding and manipulating objects which became the first tools and weapons.

The first true human beings, called Homo habilis, or 'handy man', appeared about 2.5 million years ago. They were more intelligent than the man-apes. A million years later another species, Homo erectus, or 'upright man', appeared. Homo erectus was the first to spread from Africa to Asia and later Europe. These early humans, or hominids, learned to hunt and gather food, to make shelters and fire, to communicate and to make tools. The first tools were little more than usefully-shaped pebbles but by chipping away at flint, people learnt how to create sharp cutting or scraping edges.

Modern humans, Homo sapiens sapiens, our own direct ancestors, first lived about 100,000 years ago. They were excellent tool makers and hunters. By about 35,000 years ago, they had spread all over Europe and had reached Australia. Examples of tools and cave art found by archaeologists show just how skilful Homo sapiens sapiens had become at shaping objects and looking at the world around them.

Homo sapiens sapiens (Modern man) From 15,000 years ago – worldwide

◁ *The hand axe was amongst the very first type of tool to be made. It was used not just for chopping wood and bone but also for digging up roots, cutting meat and animal skins. It was used until about 13,000 BC.*

13

THE FIRST FARMERS

For the great majority of human history, people have found their food by hunting and gathering. They hunted wild animals, such as mammoths, bison and deer, and gathered berries, nuts and roots to eat.

Meat from hunting wild animals made up about a third of prehistoric people's diet. Hunting meant that the people were nomadic. They were not based in one place but had to follow the herds of animals they hunted by moving base from season to season.

Then, about 10,000 years ago, a massive change occurred in the way people lived. People learned how to grow their own crops and to rear animals for their meat, milk and skins. Instead of having to roam farther and farther afield to find enough food to eat, people found they could grow enough food on a small patch of land to feed their families. This meant, in turn, that they had to settle in one place all year round and build permanent homes. These people were the first farmers. Their farming settlements became the first villages, which grew to become the first towns.

Plants and animals that are grown or raised by people are known as domesticated. Wheat and barley were two of the first crops to be domesticated. They had grown wild in parts of the Near East for thousands of years. The first farmers collected seeds from these wild plants and sowed them in ground dug over with deer antlers. The following year, the crop was harvested and the grain used for grinding into flour. It was used to make bread, which was baked on hot stones. Grain was also made into beer. Farmers also learned how to tame wild animals and breed them in captivity. The first domesticated animals were sheep, goats and pigs. These animals are still among the most common domesticated animals in the world.

△ These cave paintings, 10,000 years old, are from Tassili, in Algeria. They show people hunting giraffe, hippopotamus, rhinoceros and elephant. Later paintings show farmers tending herds of cattle.

▽ Life on a farm in Europe around 3000 BC was very hard work. People made storage pots from clay and fired them in a kiln. They used stone axes to fell trees and stone sickles to clear the ground and harvest their crops. They spun wool into thread and wove it into cloth.

THE FIRST TOWNS

Once people began to farm and to settle in permanent villages, the world's population grew rapidly. Towns grew up and services were established for the people of the town to use, such as roads, drainage systems and shops. Trade also grew between towns as neighbouring farmers bought and sold any surplus produce. Specialist craft workers carved figurines, made fine jewellery and produced clay pots, jars and cooking vessels. Little is known about the very first towns. The ruins of two, Jericho in Jordan and Çatal Hüyük in Turkey, however, have provided archaeologists with a fascinating glimpse into the past.

Dating from about 8000 BC, Jericho was constructed near a natural spring, which was ideal for watering farmers' fields. Wheat and barley were grown, with sheep and goats raised for their meat. Jericho also stood on an important trade route and quickly grew wealthy. At one time, 2000 people live there. To defend itself, the town was surrounded by massive stone walls, some 3 m thick and more than 5 m high. Inside the walls stood small, circular houses made of mud bricks, shaped by hand and left to bake hard in the sun. Jericho's walls were destroyed many times, by earthquakes but never by invading enemies.

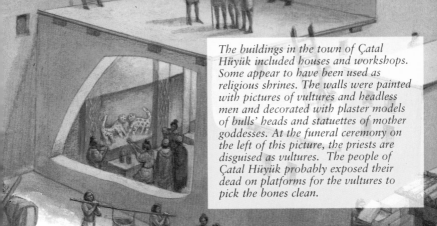

The buildings in the town of Çatal Hüyük included houses and workshops. Some appear to have been used as religious shrines. The walls were painted with pictures of vultures and headless men and decorated with plaster models of bulls' heads and statuettes of mother goddesses. At the funeral ceremony on the left of this picture, the priests are disguised as vultures. The people of Çatal Hüyük probably exposed their dead on platforms for the vultures to pick the bones clean.

The people of Çatal Hüyük were also successful farmers. Thanks to the town's position on a fertile river plain, its people grew wheat, barley and vegetables, although the town's wealth was also based mainly on trade and cattle-breeding. The town controlled the trade in obsidian, for making tools and weapons, which was mined nearby. By 6500 BC, Çatal Hüyük was flourishing and some 5000 people lived there. For safety, they lived in interconnecting, rectangular houses, with no doors. People entered their houses through holes in the roofs, reached by long, wooden ladders. The rooftops also acted as streets. If the town was attacked, the ladders were quickly removed, leaving no obvious means of entry.

△ This skull of a young woman was found in Jericho. Its eyes are set with cowrie shells. It may have been used in religious rituals, as part of some form of ancestor worship. The rest of the woman's skeleton was buried under the floor of the house.

17

MESOPOTAMIA and SUMER

One of the world's earliest civilizations grew up on the fertile plains between the rivers Tigris and Euphrates. Now situated in Iraq, this area became known as Mesopotamia, 'the land between the two rivers'. In about 5000 BC, a group of people called the Sumerians settled in the southern part of Mesopotamia.

Although the climate was hot and dry, the fertile land was ideal for growing crops and farmers soon learned how to build irrigation canals to bring water from the rivers to their fields. As more land was cultivated and more food produced, the population grew. By about 3500 BC, the original farming villages had grown into thriving towns and cities. Some of the larger settlements, such as Ur and Uruk, grew into cities, then into independent city-states. The cities were ruled by Councils of Elders. In times of war, the Council appointed a lugal, or general, to lead the army. As wars between the rival cities became more frequent, so the lugals' powers grew. From about 2900 BC, the lugals became kings and ruled for life.

In the centre of each city stood a temple to the city's patron god or goddess. The Sumerians worshipped hundreds of gods and goddesses. They believed they controlled every aspect of nature and everyday life. It was vital to

◁ *This Sumerian woman's magnificent jewellery is made from gold and silver, inlaid with precious stones, such as lapis lazuli. Sumerian craft workers made many fabulous treasures, including furniture and musical instruments. Treasures like these were discovered when the Royal Tombs at Ur were excavated.*

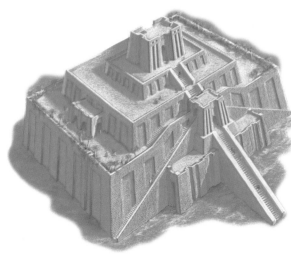

◁ This great ziggurat, or stepped temple, was built in the city of Ur by King Ur-Nammu in about 2100 BC. It was worshipped as the home of the Moon god, Nanna. The god's shrine was at the very top.

obey the gods, otherwise, they might send wars, floods and disease to punish the people.

The Sumerians were expert mathematicians and astronomers. They had two systems of counting. One was a decimal system, using the number 10, like the system we use today. The other used units of 60, for calculating time and the areas of circles. The Sumerians were the first to divide an hour into 60 minutes. They also devised a calendar and adapted the potter's wheel for transport. Their most important breakthrough, however, was the invention of writing in about 3500 BC.

The story of Gilgamesh

The Sumerians had many myths and legends about their gods and heroes. The most famous, the Epic of Gilgamesh, tells the story of Gilgamesh, a Sumerian king, and his quest to find the secret of eternal life. Gilgamesh is told of a plant growing at the bottom of the sea that will bring immortality. Gilgamesh finds the plant, but, before he can use it, it is stolen by a snake.

◁ Writing was invented in Sumer as a way of keeping temple records and merchants' accounts. The Sumerian system of writing used a series of wedge-shaped strokes to represent words. These were impressed on a tablet of wet clay by a reed pen and left to bake dry in the sun.

19

ANCIENT EGYPT

The ancient Egyptians depended on the Nile River for drinking water and irrigation, and on its annual flooding that deposited rich, silty soil along its banks. Here farmers cultivated wheat and barley (for bread and beer), flax (for linen), fruit and vegetables. They also raised cattle, sheep and goats.

△ *Hieroglyphics was the system of picture writing used in ancient Egypt. Each picture, or hieroglyph, stood for an object, image or sound. Hieroglyphs were extremely complicated so highly-trained scribes were employed to read and write them.*

The first villages of ancient Egypt were established some 7000 years ago. In time, these small settlements formed two kingdoms – Lower Egypt in the Nile Delta and Upper Egypt along the river valley. In about 3100 BC, King Menes, the ruler of Upper Egypt, united the two kingdoms and established Dynasty 1, the first dynasty (line of kings) of ancient Egypt. The king was the most powerful person in ancient Egyptian society and was worshipped as the god Horus, in human form. From about 1554 BC, the king was given the honorary title of pharaoh, from the Egyptian words per aa, which mean 'great house'. To keep the royal blood pure, the pharaoh often married a close relation, such as his half-sister. Every aspect of Egyptian life was under the pharaoh's control. The pharaoh appointed two officials, called viziers, to help him govern and collect taxes. The country was divided into 42 districts governed

▷ This gold death mask covered the face of the dead boy-king, Tutankhamun. His tomb was one of the last to be found intact and archaeologists have learnt much from its treasures inside. Tutankhamun's mummified body was wrapped in linen inside a nest of three coffins, encased in a stone sarcophagus.

on the pharaoh's behalf by officials called Nomarchs. Further officials were put in charge of the major state departments – the Treasury, the Royal Works (which supervised the building of pyramids and tombs), the Granaries, Cattle and Foreign Affairs.

The ancient Egyptians believed strongly in life after death. For a person's soul to prosper, it had to travel through the underworld called Duat and face a series of ordeals and judgements before it could progress to a better life in the next world. For the soul to travel, the ancient Egyptians believed that the body must remain intact. They learnt how to preserve bodies by drying them out, oiling and then wrapping the body in linen, before placing it in its coffin. This process is called mummification.

◁ These canopic jars stored the internal organs (such as the liver and lungs) of a dead person whose body was being mummified. The jar's stoppers were carved in the shape of the heads of protective gods and the jars stored in a special chest inside the tomb.

21

INDUS VALLEY

Around 3000 BC, another great early civilization grew up along the banks of the river Indus in ancient India (present-day Pakistan). Called the Indus Valley civilization, by 2500 BC it had reached the height of its power.

Carved Seals
Archaeologists have found a great many carved stone seals among the ruins of the Indus cities. These were used by merchants to seal their bundles of goods. Many show animals or religious scenes.

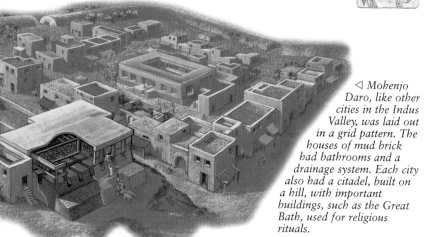

◁ *Mohenjo Daro, like other cities in the Indus Valley, was laid out in a grid pattern. The houses of mud brick had bathrooms and a drainage system. Each city also had a citadel, built on a hill, with important buildings, such as the Great Bath, used for religious rituals.*

The Indus Valley civilization was larger than either Sumer or ancient Egypt. Its two great centres were the cities of Harappa and Mohenjo Daro, each with a population of some 40,000 people. The Indus Valley civilization had a highly organized system of trade. Merchants traded grain and other agricultural produce, as well as artefacts made by the cities' artists and craft workers, for precious metals and cloth. From about 2000 BC, however, this mighty civilization began to decline. This may have been caused by terrible flooding or by the river Indus changing course so that the fertile farmland dried up. Another theory is that the people over-grazed the land, leaving it too dry and poor to support crops.

MEGALITHIC EUROPE

From about 4500 BC, people in Europe began building monuments of massive, standing stones, called megaliths. These were placed in circles or upright next to each other, with another stone laid horizontally on top.

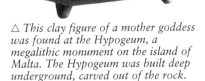

△ This clay figure of a mother goddess was found at the Hypogeum, a megalithic monument on the island of Malta. The Hypogeum was built deep underground, carved out of the rock.

△ Stonehenge in England is the most famous stone circle of all. Built in three stages, from about 2800 BC, the stones were positioned to align precisely with the rays of the Sun on Midsummer's Day. Other stones align with the phases of the Moon, which suggests that Stonehenge may have been a gigantic calendar.

△ Druids used megalithic stone circles hundreds of years after they were built. The druids were the religious leaders of the Celtic peoples of Europe.

Stones circles were laid out very carefully, according to strict mathematical rules, but no one is sure what they were used for. They may have been early observatories for studying the Sun, Moon and stars, or religious temples. Experts also think that sacrifices, both human and animal, may have taken place inside these intriguing circles of stone.

Megalithic builders also constructed stone monuments over the graves of their dead. These often took the form of long, passage-like chambers, lined with megaliths, and buried under a mound of earth, called a barrow. One tomb contained over 40 skeletons. Offerings of food and drink, pots and tools were left at the tomb entrance for the dead to use in the next world.

23

MINOANS

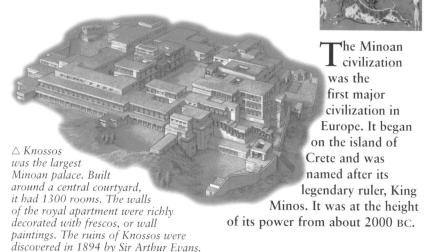

△ Knossos was the largest Minoan palace. Built around a central courtyard, it had 1300 rooms. The walls of the royal apartment were richly decorated with frescos, or wall paintings. The ruins of Knossos were discovered in 1894 by Sir Arthur Evans.

The Minoan civilization was the first major civilization in Europe. It began on the island of Crete and was named after its legendary ruler, King Minos. It was at the height of its power from about 2000 BC.

◁ Minoan pottery was very skilfully made. Minoan potters made huge clay jars, taller than a person, for storing oil, wine and grain. These jars were called pithoi.

▷ According to Greek legend, a terrible monster, half-man, half-bull, lived in a labyrinth (maze) under the palace of Knossos on Crete. It was eventually killed by the Athenian prince, Theseus.

The Minoans had a rich and glittering culture, with a highly organized society and flourishing economy. Merchants travelled far and wide throughout the Mediterranean, trading wine, grain and olive oil, grown by the island's farmers, for luxury goods, such as amber, ivory and precious metals. Each large Minoan town was built around a splendid palace, housing hundreds or even thousands of people. Apart from being royal residences, palaces acted as trading centres, where goods could be stored ready for export. They also contained shrines, workshops and living quarters for officials. By 1450 BC, however, most of the palaces had been destroyed, probably by earthquakes or volcanic eruptions, and Crete was taken over by the Mycenaeans.

MYCENAEANS

From about 1600 BC to 1100 BC the Mycenaeans dominated mainland Greece. They lived in separate, small kingdoms, although they shared the same language and beliefs. Their greatest city was Mycenae.

The Mycenaeans built their great palaces on hill tops, surrounded by massive stone walls. This type of fortified city was called an acropolis, which means 'high city' in Greek. These fortifications made their cities much easier to defend. Mycenaean society was based around farming and trade, and they founded colonies on Rhodes and Cyprus. They also seem to have been successful warriors. Many examples of armour and weapons have been found in the graves of Mycenaean kings and nobles.

△ This gold death mask has aroused fierce debate. Schliemann believes that it once covered the face of Agamemnon, the legendary king of Mycenae and hero of the Trojan War. Others disagree, believing the mask to be 300 years older.

In 1876, the German archaeologist, Heinrich Schliemann, was excavating part of Mycenae when he discovered five graves. These contained the bodies of 16 members of the Mycenaean royal family, five of whom had exquisite gold death masks covering their faces. Alongside lay priceless golden treasures, including swords, goblets and crowns.

△ The Lion Gate was the main gateway into Mycenae. Built in around 1250 BC, the two carved lions above the gate may have been symbols of the Mycenaean royal family.

25

ANCIENT CHINA

The earliest civilizations in China grew up along the banks of three major rivers – the Chang Jiang (Yangtze), Xi Jiang (West River) and Huang He (Yellow River). Farmers used the river water to irrigate their crops but they also faced the frequent risk of floods that could devastate their harvests.

From about 2205 BC, China was ruled by a series of dynasties (families). The first for which experts have reasonable evidence is the Shang Dynasty, which began in about 1766 BC. The Shang ruled China for more than 400 years. At the end of the 11th century BC, however, the Shang were conquered by the Zhou. Their rule lasted until 221 BC. During this time many wars were fought between the rival kingdoms that made up the Zhou lands, but it was also a period of economic growth and of trading success, with Chinese silk, precious jade and fine porcelain being traded abroad.

By 221 BC, the kingdoms of China had been at war for more than 250 years. Gradually, the Qin (or Ch'in), a war-like dynasty from the northwest, united the country and established the empire that gives China its name. The first emperor of the united China, Shi Huangdi, reorganized government and standardized money, weights and measures.

A road and canal network was also built to link up the various parts of the country and the Great Wall of China, built across the northern border to keep the hostile Hsung Nu people (the Huns) out. Shi Huangdi was a brilliant but ruthless general and politician, burning books and putting scholars to death because their ideas did not match his own. Despite his achievements, however, the Qin Dynasty was overthrown in 206 BC, four years after Shi Huangdi's death.

The Great Wall of China, built between 214 and 204 BC formed a huge barrier more than 2250 km long, 9 m high and wide enough for chariots to drive along the top. Thousands of peasants were sent to work on the wall. If their work was below standard, they were put to death.

AROUND 1500 BC

BEFORE 213 BC

AFTER AD 200

△ *The earliest Chinese writing is found on oracle bones used by the Shang to predict the future. By the time of the Zhou Dynasty, several thousand characters were in use. At first, the characters were drawn as picture symbols. Gradually they became more abstract in form.*

Confucius

The prophet and philosopher Confucius, born in about 551 BC, dedicated himself to teaching people how to live in peace with each other. His thoughts and teachings were incredibly influential in China until the start of the 20th century.

PHOENICIANS

The greatest traders and seafarers of the ancient world were the Phoenicians. They lived along the eastern coast of the Mediterranean (now part of Syria, Lebanon and Israel). Here, in about 1500 BC, they founded their greatest cities – Tyre, their main port, and Sidon.

The Phoenicians traded glassware, timber, cedar oil, purple-dyed cloth and ivory for silver, copper and tin. They sailed throughout the Mediterranean, venturing as far west as Britain and down the African coast.

The Phoenicians themselves were named after their costliest export, a purple-red dye made in Tyre from a type of shellfish and known as phoinos in Greek.

The Phoenicians had magnificent ships which were fast and manoeuvrable. They were excellent sailors and navigators, even though they had no accurate maps or charts. They used the winds and stars to find their way.

△ Phoenician trading ships, like the one pictured, harnessed the power of the wind with their large, square sails. Rows of oarsmen helped the ship travel in any direction. A look-out kept watch for pirates who might attempt to steal the lucrative cargo

◁ Phoenician glassware was highly prized in the ancient world. The Phoenicians perfected the art of glass-making (first developed by the Egyptians) and also invented the technique of glass-blowing. Their glassware was in much demand.

◁ The Phoenicians were the leading traders in the Mediterranean from about 1200 to 350 BC. This map shows their main trade routes and colonies.

ANCIENT AMERICA

From about 1200 BC, two great civilizations grew up in ancient America – the Olmecs in western Mexico and the Chavin along the coast of northern Peru. The Olmec civilization began in about 1500 BC in a group of villages around the Gulf of Mexico. These villages grew into larger settlements like La Venta, a major centre of Olmec culture.

△ These jade and serpentine figures were part of a group found at La Venta in 1955. The tiny figures were arranged as if they were taking part in a special ritual or ceremony. They had then been carefully buried in sand.

The Olmecs were skilled artists and craft workers. They built huge earth pyramids where religious ceremonies were held, and produced hundreds of sculptures and carvings from stone, jade and clay. The Olmecs also developed a system of writing that influenced many later cultures in the region.

The Chavin civilization began in Peru in about 1200 BC and lasted for about 1000 years. It is named after the important religious site of Chavin de Huantar which featured a huge stone temple surrounded by a maze of rooms and passageways. The Chavin culture had a great influence throughout Peru.

◁ This Chavin stone bowl is decorated with geometric patterns and swirls. Chavin craft workers produced large quantities of pots and sculptures which they traded with their neighbours.

▷ Huge stepped pyramids made of earth were built by the Olmecs. Here they worshipped their gods and performed religious ceremonies.

29

ASSYRIANS & BABYLONIANS

The Assyrians originally lived around the river Tigris (now in northern Iraq). Gaining their independence in about 2000 BC, they established a line of warrior-kings, under whose leadership they built a mighty empire, which was at its greatest during the New Assyrian Empire (around 1000–612 BC). The Assyrians were tough, fearless soldiers. Their army was huge, well organized, trained and equipped.

The Assyrian king demanded annual tributes of goods and crops from conquered people. If a city refused to pay its tribute, the city was destroyed and its people tortured or made slaves. By 612 BC, however, the Assyrian Empire had become too large and unwieldy, and it fell to the invading Medes and Babylonians.

The Assyrian kings were heads of the empire's religion, government and army. They were given grand titles, such as 'King of the Universe'. To display their wealth and power, kings built magnificent cities and palaces such as Nimrud and Nineveh.

▽ The Assyrian army used fearsome battering rams fitted to assault towers mounted on wheels to break through the city walls of their enemies.

The Hittites

The Hittites were a war-like people from Anatolia (in modern-day Turkey) feared for their military skill. They were the first to use chariots for warfare. The Hittites conquered Babylon, Mesopotamia and parts of Syria before being crushed in about 1200 BC.

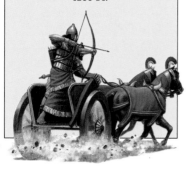

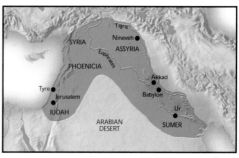

△ This map shows the Babylonian Empire under Nebuchadnezzar II. His army defeated the Egyptians to take Syria. In 586 BC, Nebuchadnezzar conquered Judah by destroying Jerusalem and transporting the survivors back to Babylon as slaves.

◁ King Nebuchadnezzar II ruled Babylon from around 602 BC to 562 BC. He captured Syria, Palestine and conquered the city of Jerusalem.

Babylonians

Babylon first grew powerful under the rule of King Hammurabi (c. 1792–1750 BC).

Hammurabi conquered neighbouring kingdoms and extended Babylon's frontiers to include Sumer and Akkad. The city of Babylon, with its magnificent temples and palaces, became the capital of the new empire. Hammurabi was a just and diplomatic ruler. He is famous for his code of law. The laws were recorded on clay tablets and stone pillars for all to see. After his death, Babylon declined in power and, over the centuries, was invaded by the Hittites, Kassites, Chaldeans and Assyrians.

Under the Assyrian king, King Nebuchadnezzar II, Babylon regained its former glory. The city was rebuilt on a grand scale, surpassing any other city in the ancient world. Its enormous city walls, some 26 m thick, featured eight massive bronze gates. The most famous, the Ishtar Gate, was used for religious parades. Babylon was finally captured by the Persians in 539 BC and became part of the mighty Persian Empire.

ANCIENT GREECE

By about 800 BC, Greece saw the rise of a new civilization that transformed the ancient world and whose influence has lasted to the present day. Ancient Greece was divided into small, independent city-states, the most important being Athens and Sparta.

▷ *Greek vases were decorated with scenes from daily life as well as stories from mythology. Much of our knowledge about the ancient Greeks comes from vases and vessels. They show what the Greeks wore and how they lived.*

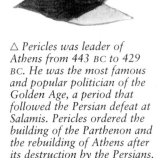

△ *Pericles was leader of Athens from 443 BC to 429 BC. He was the most famous and popular politician of the Golden Age, a period that followed the Persian defeat at Salamis. Pericles ordered the building of the Parthenon and the rebuilding of Athens after its destruction by the Persians.*

Most city-states were ruled by a group of wealthy nobles, called an oligarchy, or by an absolute ruler, called a tyrant. In about 508 BC, however, Athens introduced a new type of government, one in which all male citizens had a say. It was called democracy meaning 'rule by the people'.

Life in Sparta was different to Athens. It revolved around training every male citizen from an early age to be fearless warriors, ready to defend the city-state from foreign invaders and to keep the population under control.

The Classical Period in Greece (the time in which Greek culture was at its most splendid) lasted from about 500 BC to 336 BC. During this time Greece was involved in two great wars – the series of Persian Wars (490–449 BC) and the Peloponnesian Wars (431–404 BC). When the Persians invaded Greece in 490 BC, the city-states joined forces against the invaders and succeeded in defeating them. Greece's newly-won security did not last long. Relations between Athens and Sparta deteriorated and, in 431 BC, war broke out between them. The Peloponnesian Wars lasted for 27 years and tore the country apart.

After laying siege to Athens, the Spartans starved the Athenians into submission. In 404 BC, Athens was forced to surrender. The city never recovered from its defeat.

The ancient Greeks were great scholars, thinkers and teachers. They were amongst the first people to look for practical, scientific ways of making sense of the world around them. Drama and sport played a very important part in the lives of the ancient Greeks. Many great open-air theatres were built and sport was considered a way of both providing entertainment and keeping men fit and healthy for fighting.

Battle Ships
A turning point in the Persian Wars was the sea battle of Salamis in 480 BC. During the Persian Wars, Greek ships were used to ram enemy ships in order to sink or badly damage them. Greek archers then fired arrows at the stricken Persian crew.

◁ A hoplite, or Greek foot soldier, was the most important part of the Greek army. Each soldier carried a heavy round shield to protect his body and a long spear. The skirted tunic allowed easy movement.

ALEXANDER THE GREAT

Amid the squabbling and disunity that took hold of Greece in the aftermath of the Peloponnesian Wars, the new power of Macedonia, in the northwest, went largely unnoticed. The Macedonians took full advantage of the situation to take control of Greece.

When Philip II came to the throne in 359 BC, he united and extended the kingdom, reorganized the army and transformed Macedonia into the greatest military force of the day. In 338 BC, at the battle of Chaeronea, Philip's army gained control of Greece, uniting the Greeks and Macedonians against the mighty Persians. In 336 BC, however, Philip was assassinated and the throne passed to his 20-year-old son, Alexander. An even more brilliant leader and general than his father, it took Alexander just 13 years to conquer a vast empire that stretched from Greece in the west to India in the east. It was the largest empire in the ancient world and helped to spread Hellenistic (Greek) culture far and wide.

In 334 BC, Alexander led his army against the Persians, in order not only to conquer their lands, but to replenish his royal treasuries with their great wealth. In 333 BC, he defeated the Persian king Darius III, at the battle of Issus, and by 331 BC, had conquered the whole of Persia and become its king. To strengthen the ties between the two peoples,

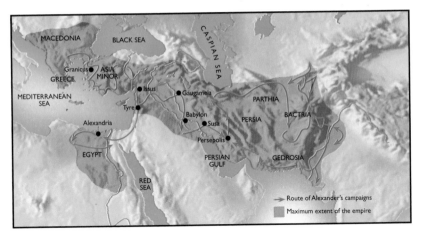

△ The map shows the extent of Alexander's empire and the routes he followed to conquer the east. During his travels, Alexander founded many cities. This helped to spread Hellenistic art and culture.

Alexander tried to include Persians in his government. He also wore Persian clothes and married a Persian princess, Roxane. Alexander went on to invade India, defeating King Porus at the battle of the river Hydaspes. It was to be his final expedition. His exhausted army refused to go any farther and Alexander was forced to retreat to Babylon. He died there, of a fever, in 323 BC, at the age of 32. After his death, his empire was fought over by his leading generals and eventually divided among them.

◁ The city of Persepolis was the magnificent capital of the Persian kings. Built by Darius I, the ruins of the city lie near Shiraz in modern-day Iran. When Alexander captured Persepolis in 331 BC, he burned Darius' splendid palace to the ground.

△ Alexander on his favourite horse, Bucephalus.

35

THE CELTS

The Celts probably first lived in France and Austria from about 600 BC. Gradually, Celtic tribes spread farther afield, across southern and western Europe, conquering the lands and settling in hill-forts and farms. They were finally defeated by the Romans and much of their territory was brought under Roman rule.

The Celts were highly skilled metal-smiths, making beautifully decorated weapons, jewellery and drinking cups. They were also gifted poets and musicians, passing down stories of their gods and history by word of mouth, as they had no written language.

▷ Safe within a hill-fort each family lived with their animals in circular wooden huts, with thatched roofs and walls covered in wattle and daub. A huge iron cooking couldron hung over the fire in the centre of the hut.

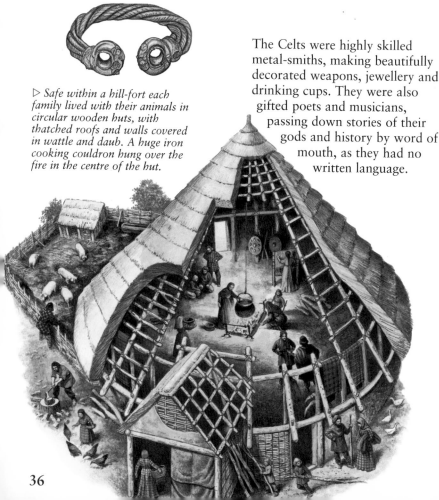

▷ **Queen Boudicca**
The Roman emperor Claudius invaded Britain in AD 43, but Celtic opposition to Roman rule did not end. In AD 60, Boudicca (or Boadicea), the queen of the Iceni, a Celtic tribe from East Anglia, led a revolt against the Romans in Britain. At first, the queen and her army enjoyed great success, taking the towns of Colchester, London and St Albans (Verulanium) and killing some 70,000 Romans. But her army was defeated in AD 61 and Boudicca killed herself by drinking poison.

Roman writers recorded details of Celtic life and culture. They reported, among other things, that the Celts worshipped many different gods and goddesses and offered sacrifices in their honour. Religious rituals and ceremonies were performed by priests, called druids. In charge of each of the Celtic tribes was a leader, or chieftain. One of the most famous was Vercingetorix, a chieftain of the Arveni, a tribe in central Gaul (France). In 52 BC, he led a successful rebellion against the Romans but was later defeated by Julius Caesar's army.

The Celts were great warriors, famed and feared for their bravery in battle. Individual warriors often fought on their own and not as part of an organized army. Wars frequently broke out between the rival Celtic tribes. This helped the Romans to defeat the Celts more easily than if they had been a unified and efficiently run military force. Many tribes built huge fortresses on the tops of hills, surrounded by massive, protective walls. Inside, the people of the tribe could live, safe from attack. Victory in battle was celebrated in grand style, with lavish feasts, hard drinking and the recital of long poems, telling of the deeds of the Celtic heroes and gods. Their greatest god was Daghdha, the 'Good God', who controlled the weather and the harvest and brought victory in battle.

THE ROMANS

According to legend, the city of Rome was founded in 753 BC by twin brothers, called Romulus and Remus. Abandoned by a wicked uncle, the twins were rescued by a she-wolf and raised by a shepherd. To repay the wolf, Romulus and Remus vowed to build a city in her honour, on the Palatine Hill where she had found them. Remus was killed in a quarrel and Romulus became the city's first king, giving Rome its name.

△ *Julius Caesar, a brilliant Roman general, held high office before leading armies in Spain, France and invading Britain in 55 BC. In 49 BC he defeated his rivals in Rome to seize power as dictator. He was assassinated by a group of senators on 15th March 44 BC.*

▷ *Metal coins were used by the Romans to buy and sell goods.*

Rome was ruled by kings until 509 BC when King Tarquin the Proud was expelled. For the next 500 years, Rome stayed a republic with power held by a law-making body of important nobles, called the Senate.

By about 50 BC, Rome had conquered most of the lands around the Mediterranean but all was not well. Rivalry between army generals and tensions between rich and poor plunged Rome into a bloody civil war. The old republic crumbled. In 27 BC, Octavian, the adopted son of Julius Caesar, became the first Roman emperor, charged with restoring peace and stability to

◁ *This fresco, or wall painting, comes from Pompeii, which was destroyed in AD 79 by a volcanic eruption. Many buildings were amazingly preserved under the ash and lava that smothered the town.*

Rome. Under the rule of the emperors, Rome reached its greatest extent, ruling over much of Europe, North Africa and the Near East.

The amazing expansion and success of the Roman Empire was due largely to its army, the best trained and equipped in the world. Soldiers were paid good wages and joined up for 20 to 25 years. Soldiers were grouped into units, called legions, each made up of about 5000 men. Centurions commanded groups of 80 men.

Roman society was divided into citizens and non-citizens. All citizens were allowed to vote in elections and to serve in the army. Non-citizens included people who lived outside Rome itself and slaves. All the hardest, dirtiest jobs on which the Roman Empire heavily relied were performed by a vast workforce of slaves owned by the government or by wealthy citizens.

Hannibal

From 264 BC to 146 BC, Rome and Carthage fought for control of the Mediterranean. In 218 BC, the Carthaginian general, Hannibal, led a surprise attack by marching over the Alps and into Italy with 35,000 men and 37 elephants. Carthage, however, was finally defeated.

EMPIRES OF INDIA

In about 321 BC, a young prince, Chandragupta Maurya, founded the first Indian empire. It stretched right across northern India, from the Hindu Kush in the west to Bengal in the east.

Chandragupta's grandson, Ashoka, extended the empire still farther, until most of India came under Mauryan rule. In 260 BC, and sickened by the bloodshed he had seen in battle, Ashoka converted to Buddhism. He promoted policies of peace and religious tolerance and travelled throughout his empire, listening to ordinary people and trying to improve their lot – an unusual step for a ruler of that time.

After the collapse of the Mauryan empire in about 185 BC, India was divided into a number of smaller, independent states and kingdoms. AD 320 saw the rise of the Gupta empire which ruled over northern India for 200 years. During this time, the region extended its trading links and enjoyed a period where arts, literature, science, medicine and mathematics all flourished.

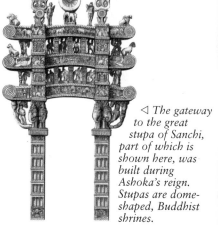

◁ *The gateway to the great stupa of Sanchi, part of which is shown here, was built during Ashoka's reign. Stupas are dome-shaped, Buddhist shrines.*

Hinduism

The Hindu religion began more than 4000 years ago. Under Ashoka, Buddhism became the major religion of India. Hinduism enjoyed a revival under the Guptas although Buddhism remained very strong. Today, more than three-quarters of Indians are Hindu.

◁ *Emperor Ashoka Maurya, one of India's greatest ever rulers, has had a lasting effect on modern India. In Sarnath, where the Buddha first taught, Ashoka erected a tall pillar topped with four lions and four wheels, the symbols of Buddhism. Today, this is the national emblem of India.*

40

THE MIDDLE AGES

The period from about 500 to 1400 in Europe is known as the Middle Ages, or the medieval period. It was an age of wars and conquests and a time when religion dominated most peoples' lives. During this period, China's civilization was far in advance of the rest of the world. Africa and America saw the emergence of strong, well-organized empires based on trade, while the spread of Islam brought a new way of life to a vast area.

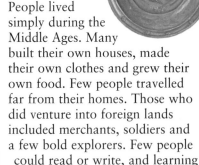

People lived simply during the Middle Ages. Many built their own houses, made their own clothes and grew their own food. Few people travelled far from their homes. Those who did venture into foreign lands included merchants, soldiers and a few bold explorers. Few people could read or write, and learning was passed down by word of mouth. In Europe, the monasteries were centres of learning, while in Asia the Chinese and Arabs led the way in science and technology, medicine and astronomy.

BYZANTIUM

For over 500 years, the Roman Empire brought a unique way of life to a vast area of land. In 476, the western half of the empire collapsed, overrun by invading German tribes. In the east, however, Roman rule continued to flourish under what is called the Byzantine Empire.

The old Greek city-port of Byzantium (modern-day Istanbul in Turkey) was the centre of the eastern Roman Empire. The Romans named it Constantinople after the first Byzantine emperor, Constantine. It became the seat of the Byzantine emperors and the centre of the eastern Christian church. Within the Byzantine Empire, ancient Greek and Roman culture and learning was preserved. The Byzantines appreciated music, poetry and art, and decorated churches, such as

Hagia Sophia in Constantinople, with complex and finely detailed frescoes (wall paintings) and mosaics (pictures made from hundreds of tiny pieces of glass or stone fitted together).

The Byzantine Empire reached its peak in the 500s, under the emperor Justinian. His general, Belisarius, won many battles and expanded the empire to include Italy, Greece, Turkey, parts of Spain, North Africa and Egypt. Justinian's wife, Theodora, helped govern the empire and was almost

▷ This map shows the Eastern Roman Empire at its height, in the 500s. From their capital at Byzantium, the Eastern Roman emperors controlled the eastern Mediterranean and the southern Mediterranean coast as far as North Africa and Spain.

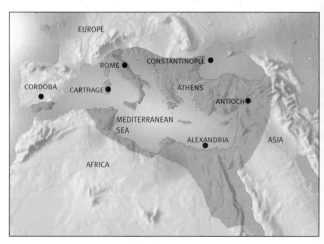

as powerful as her husband. Justinian's code of laws later formed the basis for legal systems in many European countries.

Most of the people were farmers, living in small villages. Traders came to sell goods in the towns. Constantinople was a busy port and meeting place for peoples from as far away as Spain, China and Russia.

Warlike invaders from the east threatened this last Roman Empire. Justinian's reign was a last flourish of imperial power. The invaders carved off chunks of territory and after Justinian's death in 565, Byzantium was never as strong again. The empire was weakened by frequent wars and eventually fell to the Turks in 1453.

△ *This beautiful Byzantine mosaic is of the Magi, or wise men, visiting Jesus. It dates from the 6th century and can be found in the Church of Sant' Appolinare Nuovo in Ravenna, Italy.*

▽ *Chariot races were not just entertainment. Watched by the emperor, howling mobs in the Hippodrome cheered for Blues or Greens to show their support for one of the rival political factions in Byzantium.*

THE ISLAMIC EMPIRE

In the early 7th century, the Arab peoples were not united. They all worshipped different gods and lived by farming or crossing the desert on camels to trade. Then, in about 610, an Arab merchant named Muhammad began to preach a new religion, Islam, which means 'submission to the will of God'. According to Muslim belief, Muhammad was sent by God as a messenger. Muhammad had several religious revelations and his teachings were written down in the Koran, the holy book of Islam. He set out religious laws that included five daily prayers and a month of fasting.

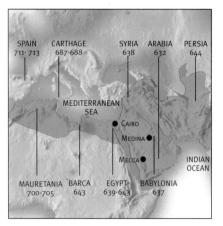

◁ *This map shows Islamic conquests beyond Arabia began in 634. In 81 years the new religion had spread from Persia in the east to southern Spain in the west.*

SPAIN
711· 713

CARTHAGE
687-688

SYRIA
638

ARABIA
632

PERSIA
644

MEDITERRANEAN
SEA

● CAIRO

MEDINA ●

MECCA ●

INDIAN
OCEAN

MAURETANIA
700-705

BARCA
643

EGYPT
639-643

BABYLONIA
637

▽ *A European view of life behind the palace doors of a Muslim ruler. Islam permitted a man to have four wives but only if he guaranteed to treat them all equally. It also gave women rights to property, to custody of their children, and to maintenance after divorce.*

Muhammad is presented as reflecting an ideal: courageous, resolute, yet gentle. His teachings helped create a state from a collection of Arab tribes. The religion united the peoples of Arabia to eventually form a huge Arab empire which stretched almost from China to the border of France.

When Muhammad died in 632, he left a daughter, Fatima, but no son or instruction on who should succeed him. Arguments between different groups over the principles of succession started which have not been settled to this day.

After Muhammad's death, his followers spread Islam by preaching and by conquest. The Persian and Byzantine empires were too weak to withstand the attacks, and Syria, Egypt and Afghanistan were also conquered. By the 700s, Muslims controlled most of the Middle East and North Africa. Muslims from Morocco invaded southern Spain, but any further advance into Europe was halted by the Frankish army of Charles Martel in 732.

In the mid 700s, Abu al-Abbas, a descendant of Muhammad, founded a new dynasty, the Abbasids, with its capital based in Baghdad (in what is now Iraq). Baghdad became the centre of a rich new Islamic civilization, blending many cultures with Islamic places of worship, called mosques, stretching from Afghanistan to Spain.

△ *A Muslim astronomer. Muslim astronomers observed the stars. Scholars preserved the ideas of the Greek astronomer, Ptolemy, about the universe.*

Toleration of Jews
Muslims, Christians and Jews got on well in many parts of the Islamic world. Muslim rulers tolerated Jewish and Christian minority communities in their lands because in the teachings and beliefs of the three religions there is much that is shared and especially a faith in one true God.

THE MAYA

The Maya lived in Central America. Their civilization lasted more than 700 years and they built huge cities with magnificent stone temples that can still be seen today.

The Maya were at their most powerful from about 200 to 900, although their culture lasted until the Spanish conquest of Central America in the early 1500s. The Maya lived in organized city-states, each with its own ruler who controlled trade in obsidian, cacao, cotton and other goods and fought wars with neighbouring city-states. Bird-catchers traded colourful feathers, which were used to make headdresses. In the countryside, farmers cleared forest land and terraced the hillsides to grow beans, corn and squash. They raised turkeys and kept bees, but the Maya had no domestic animals other than dogs and no vehicles other than toy carts.

The largest Mayan city was Tikal, in what is now Guatemala, with a population of 60,000. Crowds filled the large squares around the pyramid-temples to watch ceremonies conducted by priests, who studied the heavens to predict eclipses of the Moon and Sun. Religion was important to the Mayas and, to win favours from their many gods, they made sacrifices. Mostly they sacrificed animals but they also threw human victims into sacred wells. The Maya played a sacred ball-game, in which players hit a rubber ball through a stone ring with their hips.

The Maya invented the first writing in America, and wrote

△ The Maya settled in a region of what is now Mexico from the Yucatan peninsula in the north to the Pacific coast in the south. Each of the 50 states had its own ruler and sacred city, such as Chichén Itzá, Tikál and Copán.

▽ A jadeite mask made by a Mayan artist and possibly used by a priest during a religious ceremony. Jadeite is a hard, green gemstone which was highly valued.

A CHICHEN ITZA
B MAYAPAN
C IXMAL
D TIKAL
E COPAN

codexes (folding books) with pages of tree bark, three of which survive. They also set up tall carved stones to commemorate dates and important events. Their number system was based on 20 (not 10, like ours) and they had two calendars, one with 360 days and another (associated with the Mayan gods) that had 260 days. Many people in Mexico still speak Mayan languages today.

▽ A Mayan ruler enters his city on a litter. Everyone had to worship the ruler like a god and offer him tribute in the form of goods (such as corn) or work (such as temple building). Sculptures and wall-paintings celebrated royal triumphs, listed family trees and linked kings with the mighty gods.

47

CHARLEMAGNE AND THE HOLY ROMAN EMPIRE

Charles I, King of the Franks was known as Charlemagne (Charles the Great). He founded the Holy Roman Empire and was regarded by many people as the ideal ruler. He is still well known today.

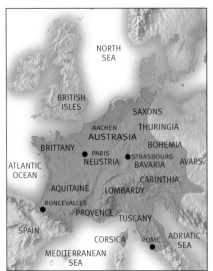

▽ Charlemagne's empire grew from the lands of Austrasia (France and Germany) he inherited from his father Pepin in 768 and his brother in 771 (in orange on the map). The Frankish empire was at its largest soon after (orange and red).

Charlemagne was born in 742. His father was King Pepin, son of the famous soldier, Charles Martel, and founder of the new Frankish ruling family (later called the Carolingian dynasty, after Charlemagne). In 768 Pepin died, leaving his kingdom to his sons Carloman and Charlemagne. When Carloman died, Charlemagne was left in sole control.

Charlemagne had learned much from his ruthless warrior father and led his armies out of the Frankish homeland of France into what are now the Netherlands, Germany and Italy. He was a Christian and wherever he conquered non-believers, such as the Saxons of Germany and the Avars of Hungary, he forced them to become Christians and to take part in mass baptisms.

There was more to Charlemagne than simply waging wars of conquest.

▽ *The iron lance of the Holy Roman emperors was a holy relic as well as a symbol of power. Around the spearpoint is a gold sheath stretched over a nail reputedly from Jesus's cross, as recorded by the inscription that runs along it.*

Although uneducated, he had great respect for scholarship. His capital at Aachen was the glittering centre of his empire, with a splendid palace and heated swimming pool, but the emperor himself dressed and lived simply. He spoke Latin and Greek, had books read aloud to him and invited famous scholars like Alcuin of York to his court to train teachers and to transcribe ancient Roman writings.

Charlemagne's position as Europe's strongest leader was recognized in 800 when the Pope crowned him Holy Roman emperor. After he died in 814, his empire was weakened by attacks and civil wars, and was soon split between his three grandsons. Charlemagne's life story was written by a scholar named Einhard, at the request of the emperor's son, Louis the Pious. His fame made him a legend and the Holy Roman Empire that he founded lasted in one form or another until 1806.

◁ *Charlemagne's tomb at the imperial capital, Aachen, dates from 1215 and is decorated in gold and precious stones. Artists working 400 years after Charlemagne's death had written descriptions of his appearance, but no likeness of him to copy.*

THE VIKINGS

The Vikings' homelands in Scandinavia had little good farmland. Most Vikings lived close to the sea, tending small fields, keeping sheep and cattle and catching fish. All Vikings worked very hard with the leader of each community, the richest landowner, or jarl, who was expected to share his wealth with his followers by feasting and entertaining them in his great hall. Viking traders travelled on horseback to market towns where they traded furs, walrus ivory and reindeer antlers for weapons, jewels and pottery.

The Vikings grew rich through trade and agriculture and as the population increased, farmland became increasingly scarce. From the late 700s, the Vikings began to venture from Scandanavia to land on the coasts of western Europe in search of better farmland and more riches. Viking longships were fast and strong enough to cross oceans. Vikings were brave and fierce fighters using their favourite weapons – iron swords and axes. They raided monasteries and towns, carrying off slaves and booty.

The Vikings were also looking to seize land. Viking attacks on England began in 787, and from 865 Vikings from Denmark had begun to settle in eastern England, the Orkney and Shetland islands and Ireland. Vikings attacked what is now France, but were bought off with the gift of Normandy in 911. Sailing west into the Atlantic Ocean, Norwegian Vikings settled in Iceland (874) and Greenland (982) and landed in North America (c. 1000).

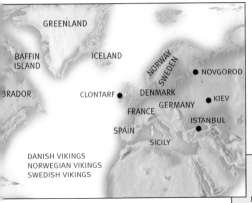

◁ *Viking trade routes extended from Scandinavian towns like Hedeby (Denmark) to Jorvik (York), Dublin, Iceland and the Baltic. Vikings travelled as far east as Novgorod (Russia), Baghdad and Istanbul.*

Swedish Vikings travelled as far east as the Black Sea and into the Mediterranean where they reached Baghdad and Constantinople. Goods from such exotic places found their way back to Viking towns such as Jorvik (York) in England and Dublin in Ireland.

Where Vikings settled they often mingled with the local people. In England, King Alfred of Wessex led the fight against the invaders, but Viking settlements in eastern England (the Danelaw) left a permanent legacy in customs, laws, place names and language. Viking words, for example, include knife and calf.

Weighing coins

Vikings valued coins by weight, so many traders carried balance scales to check or show that money was good. Small lead weights such as those below were used to check coins. Small scales for weighing silver have been found at Jorvik and other Viking settlements.

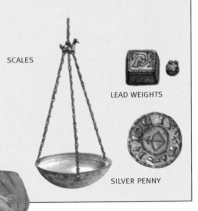

SCALES

LEAD WEIGHTS

SILVER PENNY

◁ *Viking farmers made the most of their household items, including tools, clothes and furniture. They also made things to sell at market. Wood, ivory, deer antler, leather, pottery, bone and iron were common materials. Vikings wore hard-wearing clothes made from woollen or linen cloth. Women wore a linen dress with a wool tunic on top, fastened by brooches.*

51

THE CRUSADES

Jerusalem was an important place of pilgrimage for Jews, Muslims and Christians but in 1095 Muslim Turks who held the holy city barred Christians. This angered both the eastern Christian church (based in Constantinople) and the western Christian church (based in Rome) and in 1096 a European army joined a Byzantine army from Constantinople to free Jersualem. The First Crusade, or war of the cross, was launched.

▷ Transport ships were loaded with soldiers and equipment bound for the Crusades. Special groups of knights were founded to protect Christians on their journey including the Knights Templars.

△ Crusaders found the weather in the lands around Jerusalem incredibly hot. They soon learned from the Muslim soldiers and wore airy, loose robes over their armour.

Their leaders were inspired by religious faith and by a less spiritual desire to increase territory and wealth. In three years they captured Jerusalem and went on to set up Christian kingdoms in Palestine. But none of the seven later crusades fought over the following 200 years for control of the Holy Land matched this success.

In the end, the Crusaders failed to win back the Holy Land. Yet, Europeans learned more about Eastern art and science, foods and medicine. Contacts and trade between Europe and Asia grew during the Crusades.

◁ Once Crusaders had conquered lands, they built strong castles to defend them. These featured massive gates and steep ramparts from which castle defenders fired arrows and threw rocks and boiling oil. Castle defenders faced starvation and bombardment by giant catapults when an attack laid siege.

THE MONGOL EMPIRE

The Mongols lived on the plains of central Asia, from the Ural mountains to the Gobi Desert. They were nomads, wandering with their herds and living in portable tent-homes called yurts. Their leaders were chiefs called khans. In 1206, Chief Temujin brought all the tribes under his rule and was proclaimed Genghis Khan, meaning lord of all. In a lifetime of conquest, he seized an empire that stretched from the Pacific Ocean to the River Danube, the largest in history.

Mongol armies sent a shockwave of fear and panic around Asia and Europe – some Church leaders claimed that the Mongols were sent by God to punish Christians for their sins. Mogul warriors were infamous for their speed and ferocity in battle and their merciless slaughtering of the inhabitants of captured settlements. The Mongols continued their advance after the death of Ghengis Khan in 1237. They only turned back when Ogadai Khan, son of Ghengis, died in 1241.

◁ Although ruthless in battle, Genghis Khan kept the peace in his empire. He wiped out whole cities yet trade flourished and all religions were tolerated.

▽ Mongols preferred to fight on horseback, travelling with five horses each. Warriors controlled their horses with their feet, leaving their hands free to shoot bows and hurl spears. Mongol cavalry charges usually overwhelmed their enemies.

THE BLACK DEATH

The Black Death was the most horrific natural disaster of the Middle Ages. It was bubonic plague passed to humans from infected rats through flea bites. The name 'Black Death' came from the black spots that appeared on victims. Many people died the same day they fell ill. No medieval doctor knew why the Black Death struck or how to cure it.

The plague came to Europe from a diseased Mongol army fighting an Italian force in Crimea (southern Russia). The Italians sailed home carrying the plague with them. The Black Death raged from China to Scandinavia. As many as a third of the population of Europe died. The Church lost many priests, the only educated men of the time. Repeated plague attacks throughout the 14th and 15th centuries left Europe short of labour and led to much unrest amongst workers including uprisings in France in 1358 and the Peasants' Revolt in England, led by Wat Tyler in 1381.

◁ This map shows how the Black Death spread. As early as 1346 Europeans heard reports of a plague of terrible fury raging in China and India.

- 1347
- 1348
- 1349
- 1350

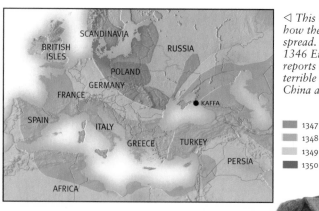

▷ Many people fled, leaving the sick to die, but some brave people stayed to care for the victims. Houses were marked with crosses to show where the disease had struck.

THE HUNDRED YEARS WAR

Edward III became king of England in 1327. He believed he also had a claim to the French throne so, in 1337, he declared war on France. War between England and France lasted on and off until 1453. Edward's forces won notable victories on land and at sea but by 1360, he gave up his claim in return for land.

Years of truce followed until Henry V renewed the claim and led his troops into France. In 1415, they defeated a much larger French army at Agincourt. To make peace Henry married the French king's daughter, but he died in 1422 and the fighting continued. The French were inspired by a peasant girl named Joan of Arc (1412–1431) who claimed to hear voices from God. She fought until the English caught her and burned her at the stake as a witch. Under the weak rule of Henry VI, the divided English lost Paris, Rouen and by 1453, all French territory except Calais.

▽ The English hoped the death of Joan of Arc would end French resistance, but, in fact, it was the French who were inspired to victory. By 1453 only Calais was left in English hands, and Joan's dreams for France had come true.

◁ Soldiers fought with halberd (far left), longbow, primitive cannon, and crossbow. Only knights, such as England's Black Prince, wore full armour.

MING CHINA

In the 14th century, the Mongols were driven out of China and a Buddhist monk founded the Ming Dynasty which ruled China for almost 300 years.

▽ *A powerful Chinese artillery crossbow like this could fire an arrow up to 200 metres, and pierce a wooden shield. The Chinese also developed gunpowder rockets and bombs, which they first used about* AD 1000.

△ *Chinese soldiers fight against invading Japanese samurai. In the 1590s the Japanese tried to invade Korea, which the Chinese regarded as their allies.*

Chinese self-confidence and power reasserted itself with a strong army built to withstand foreign attacks. From 1421, the Ming emperors lived in the Forbidden City in Beijing, a complex of palaces and temples to which no foreigners and very few Chinese were admitted. In the early 1400s, Chinese ships made voyages as far as Africa and Arabia until the government banned voyages overseas.

Ming emperors established efficient governments, abolished slavery and redistributed wealth from rich to poor. China entered a long period of peace and prosperity. Emperors sponsored the arts, so making the Ming period one of great creativity. China's first contacts with European traders began in the 1500s, when Portuguese ships arrived. Western traders were eager to buy Chinese porcelain, silk and a new drink, tea, which first reached Europe in 1610.

◁ *Italian missionary Matteo Ricci learned the language and customs of China. He arrived in China in 1583 and visited the emperor in Beijing in 1607.*

EXPLORATION & TRADE

The 1400s mark the end of the Middle Ages. In Europe, the new ideas of the Renaissance and Reformation transformed the way people thought about themselves and the world.

Constantinople fell in 1453, ending the last traces of the old Roman Empire, printing began in the 1450s and in 1492, Colombus voyaged to the Americas. People in America, Africa and Asia had greater contact with Europe. Europeans increased their power in the world through trade, using new technology such as cannons and muskets, and through a restless search for new lands and wealth. By the 1600s, several European countries had established permanent colonies overseas.

This period also saw a new freedom of thought challenging old beliefs in religion, science and government. Religious quarrels led to bitter wars and there were power struggles between kings and parliaments, as democratic government slowly developed. Startling advances in science, from the telescope and microscope to the ideas of great scientists such as Copernicus, Newton and Galileo, challenged previous thinking.

THE RENAISSANCE

The Renaissance was a rebirth of interest in the art and learning of ancient Greece and Rome and many historians say that it marked the end of the Middle Ages and the beginning of our modern world. It began in northern Italy in the 14th century and spread throughout Europe, changing the way Europeans saw themselves and how they thought about the world.

The Renaissance began in the universities and monasteries of Italy, where people rediscovered old manuscripts in Latin and Greek on science, art and literature. Some of these manuscripts were brought to Italy by Greek scholars fleeing Constantinople after that city's fall to the Ottoman Turks in 1453. Scholars tried to understand Greek and Roman beliefs, which placed more emphasis on the significance of human life on Earth rather than on an afterlife. In literature, great Italian poets such as Petrarch began to explore human emotion. By the early 1500s, three painters of genius – Leonardo da Vinci, Michelangelo and Raphael – were at the height of their powers, bringing a new energy and realism to art while architects designed new and elegant buildings that echoed the classical styles of ancient Greece and Rome.

△ *A print workshop in Denmark, about 1600. The technology of printing with a screw press and metal type spread throughout Europe. Books were printed cheaply in many languages, and read by more people, eager for information.*

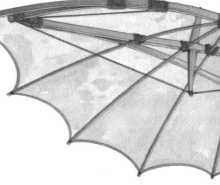

58

▷ The great dome of Florence Cathedral in Italy, designed by Filippo Brunellschi, the first major architect of the Italian Renaissance.

The Renaissance was fuelled by new technology. Printing with movable type, developed by Johannes Gutenberg in Germany, made books cheaper and more plentiful, so new ideas could be read by more people. Some new ideas were astounding, such as the revolutionary suggestion by a Polish scientist, Nicolas Copernicus, that the Sun and not the Earth was the centre of the Solar System.

The Renaissance changed the Western world forever.

▷ Dante Alighieri was one of the most famous creative figures of the era. Dante wrote in his own language, Italian, and not Latin, the language of scholars. His poem The Divine Comedy explored love, death and faith.

◁ A flying machine drawn, but never built, by the Italian Leonardo da Vinci. This sketch shows a kind of ornithopter, a machine that would flap its wings, like a bird. As well as being an artistic genius, Leonardo was a visionary, devising several futuristic machines.

THE AZTECS

The Aztecs were fierce warriors with an empire that eventually spanned Mexico. They dominated their neighbours in Central America by fighting constant wars. Conquered peoples were forced to pay taxes to the Aztec emperor and many of their number were taken for sacrifice.

The Aztecs were very skilled in sculpture, poetry, music and engineering. They worshipped the Sun as the giver of all life, and each year priests sacrificed thousands of victims to the Sun-god. Aztec farmers grew corn, beans and tomatoes, and Aztec merchants traded throughout the empire. Their capital, Tenochtitlan, was founded in 1325 on an island in the middle of Lake Texcoco, which is now the site of modern-day Mexico City. Tenochtitlan was a walled city of 100,000 people.

In 1519 Spanish treasure-seekers led by Hernando Cortés attacked the Aztecs. The Aztec emperor Montezuma II was taken prisoner and the warriors' spears and clubs were no match for Spanish guns. By 1521 the Aztec Empire was finished.

△ This sacrificial knife with a blade of obsidian was used by temple priests to cut open the bodies of victims in sacrifices to the gods. The Aztecs believed that the hearts and blood of the victims nourished the gods which would ensure bountiful harvests and good fortune.

Aztec clothing
The Aztec ruling class wore jaguar skins and headdresses made from the tail feathers of the quetzal, a bird sacred to the Aztecs. Poor people wore simple clothes made from plant fibres.

THE INCAS

The Incas took over from the Chimu as rulers of the Andes mountains of South America. Their civilization reached its peak in the 1400s under the ruler Pachacuti. From the capital city, Cuzco, Pachacuti and his successors expanded the Incan Empire to include parts of Chile, Bolivia and Ecuador. The Incas built stone cities without any form of mortar or cement and fine roads for trade. Farmers terraced the mountain slopes to grow corn, cotton and potatoes. Although they didn't have money, writing or wheeled vehicles, the Incas' many skills included music, bridge-building and medicine.

△ A mosaic mask made from mussel shells. Masks of gods' faces were worn by Inca priests for ceremonies, and were often richly decorated.

△ A gold raft depicting El Dorado, a legendary ruler whose body was said to be dusted with gold every year. Such tales aroused the greed of European invaders.

In the 1530s a Spanish expedition led by Francisco Pizarro arrived to seek gold. The Europeans were impressed by Cuzco with its palaces and temples, sanitation and water supply, and the huge fortress of Sacsahuaman. Massively outnumbered, the Spaniards relied on horses and guns, both new to the Incas. The Inca armies lost their leader Atahualpa, and were swiftly defeated, although resistance continued from scattered mountain forts, such as Machu Picchu, until 1572.

VOYAGES of DISCOVERY

In the late 1400s and 1500s, Europeans set out to explore the oceans. Building stronger ships capable of longer voyages, they went in search of trade, new lands and treasure.

When the Byzantine Empire fell to the Ottoman Turks in 1453, the old trade links by land between Europe and Asia were cut. Europeans had to find an alternative way to get to the spice-producing islands and that, coupled with a sense of adventure, prompted many to set sail.

The Portuguese were the first to go exploring. The Portuguese prince, Henry the Navigator, took a keen interest in shipbuilding and navigation. He directed Portuguese sailors west into the Atlantic and south to explore the west coast of Africa, where they set up forts and traded in gold and ivory. Spanish, French, Dutch and English sailors followed. Instead of sailing east, some sailed west hoping to find a route to India. One famous voyage was made by Christopher Columbus, the first 15th century explorer to cross the Atlantic and return. Portugal and Spain began to settle and plunder the Americas, dividing it between them by treaty. By 1517 the Portuguese had reached China and nearly 30 years later they arrived in Japan.

The ships used by the explorers were small, but more seaworthy than the clumsy vessels of the Middle Ages. They used a selection of sails for easier steering and greater manoeuvrability. Sailors had only crude maps and

ASTROLABE

△ Navigators used the cross-staff and astrolabe to fix their ships' position by the Sun and stars. The magnetic compass pointed North, but was not always reliable.

CROSS-STAFF

COMPASS

◁ *Philip II became king of Spain in 1556 and ruled until 1598. A devout Catholic, he encouraged his sailors and soldiers to explore and plunder, and convert to Christianity the 'heathen' peoples they conquered. During his reign, overseas trade and conquests brought fabulous wealth to Spain.*

▽ *Arabic script on Spanish stonework, part of the legacy Muslim craftworkers left in Southern Spain.*

simple instruments to guide them on voyages lasting many months.

In 1519 a Portuguese captain, Ferdinand Magellan, set out from Spain with five ships. They sailed around South America, across the Pacific Ocean to the Philippines (where Magellan was killed in a fight with local people) and across the Indian Ocean to Africa. Only one ship found its way home to Spain, becoming the first to sail completely around the world.

New World Foods

As well as gold and silver treasures, European explorers brought back many new foods from the Americas. Potatoes, tomatoes and peppers, turkeys and maize were all unknown in Europe before 1500. Chocolate was brought to Spain from Mexico in 1520.

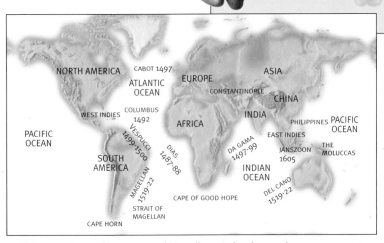

△ *This map shows the voyages of Magellan, Columbus and Da Gama. Their voyages revealed that the world was larger than ancient European geographers had believed. They sailed across oceans and landed on continents unknown earlier.*

THE REFORMATION

The Renaissance aimed to restore church practice closer to the Old and New Testaments. These changes in thinking led to the Reformation – a challenge to the established Christian Church in western Europe.

▽ *King Henry VIII made himself head of the Church of England to gain a divorce. He was not, in fact, a supporter of Protestant beliefs.*

The Renaissance led to writers from the time before Christ being read again, and their ideas inspired a new philosophy known as humanism – the belief that humans were in control of their own destinies. Humanism arose at a time of growing discontent over the way the western Christian Church was run. In 1517 Martin Luther, a German monk, protested publicly at what he saw as the Church's theological corruption and called for reform. His campaign began what is known as the Reformation and led to the formation of the Protestant Church as his ideas were taken up and spread by rebels in other countries such as Ulrich Zwingli in Switzerland and John Calvin in France.

The new technology of printing spread these new ideas. The Bible, which previously had been available only in Latin, the language of scholars, was translated into local languages for all to read. Some rulers used discontent with the church to further their own affairs. Henry VIII of England, for example, wanted his marriage to Catherine of Aragon dissolved. He asked the Pope for a divorce, but when the Pope refused, Henry broke with the Church in Rome as a means to get his own way.

From 1545 the Catholic Church fought back with a movement known as the Counter Reformation, sending out Jesuit priests to campaign against the spread of Protestantism and convert the peoples of the Spanish Empire. The split between Christians in western Europe led to wars as countries struggled with new religious alliances. Catholics and Protestants persecuted one another, often in the cruellest ways. As religious disputes in Europe continued into the 1600s, some people left Europe and sought religious freedom in the new world of America.

▷ Martin Luther believed that people were saved by faith alone, that the Bible was central to that faith, and that church services should be in everyday languages, not in Latin.

▽ The Spanish sent the Armada against England in 1588 to restore Catholic rule. An English fireship attack off Calais helped fight off the planned invasion, and the great fleet was eventually wrecked and scattered by storms around the coasts of northern Britain.

THE OTTOMAN EMPIRE

The Ottomans captured Constantinople in 1453 and renamed it Istanbul where it became the centre of a Muslim empire that, at its peak, stretched from Algeria to Arabia and from Egypt to Hungary. Much of the empire's expansion came during the rule of Suleiman I (1520–1566). By 1529 the Turkish army was outside the city walls of Vienna and looked likely to burst into western Europe. However, the siege of Vienna was lifted.

▷ *The Ottoman sultan Suleiman I made the Ottoman Empire a respected and feared power, not just in the Middle East but in Europe as well.*

▽ *The Battle of Lepanto in 1571 was fought in the Gulf of Corinth between large Turkish and Christian fleets. The Turks were defeated and lost about 20,000, the Christians 8,000.*

Suleiman also tried three times to conquer Persia which from 1501 was under the rule of the Safavids. Here the people were Shiites, not Sunni Muslims as in the Ottoman Empire.

Wars between the two empires continued throughout the 16th century and helped to stop the Ottoman Empire advancing into Europe.

Until the battle of Lepanto in 1571, Ottoman fleets of galleys (oared warships) controlled the Mediterranean Sea and Turkish pirates, such as the fearsome Barbarossa (Khayr ad-Din Pasha), raided ports, captured merchant ships and carried off Christians to be slaves.

MUGHAL INDIA

The Mughal Dynasty ruled India for nearly three hundred years. Its founder, Babur, was a Muslim chieftain from Afghanistan who captured the city of Samakand and moved on into Northern India. Babur's grandson, Akbar, came to power at just 13 but proved to be an outstanding ruler. A great military leader and skilful diplomat, Akbar maintained and enlarged his empire. He captured Bengal and gained much wealth. Akbar was also famed as a wise and just ruler who tolerated all religions. On his death in 1605, he was succeeded by his son, Jahangir who in turn was succeeded by his son Shah Jahan.

Shah Jahan's son, Aurangzeb, was the last great Mughal ruler. He expanded the empire and taxed non-Muslim subjects. He also destroyed many Hindu shrines. After his death in 1707 the Mughal Empire began to break up.

△ The Taj Mahal was built between 1631 and 1648 for Shah Jahan's favourite wife. 20,000 workers and artists created this beautiful white marble building.

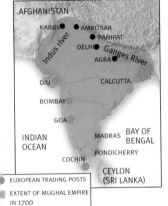

EUROPEAN TRADING POSTS

EXTENT OF MUGHAL EMPIRE IN 1700

△ This is a map of the Mughal Empire. Akbar organized an efficient land tax system to help govern his vast empire.

◁ This 1568 painting shows Akbar's soldiers, equipped with firearms, storming an enemy fortress. War elephants were used like tanks by armies in India during Akbar's brilliant wars of conquest.

67

AFRICAN EMPIRES

Africa in 1500 was a continent with many kingdoms and empires. The richest African rulers commanded trade in gold, ivory and slaves. European traders were attracted to these goods and tales of wondrous kingdoms in the heart of the continent. The strongest was Songhai, a Muslim kingdom that controlled trade across the Sahara Desert.

Songhai rule lasted until 1591 when it was overthrown by Moroccans. Another Muslim empire stretched through parts of modern-day Chad, Cameroon, Nigeria, Niger and Libya. This was Kanem-Bornu, an empire that thrived on trade between northern and southern Africa and reached its peak under Idris Alawma from about 1570.

In northeast Africa was Ethiopia, a Christian empire in the heart of Muslim Africa. Europeans heard tantalising tales of its legendary Christian ruler, Prester John. Here, and to the south, Africans lived by farming and cattle-herding. For some 400 years until its decline in 1500, a kingdom based at Great Zimbabwe in central Africa prospered. It used copper and iron and traded in gold with Sofala on the east coast of Africa (present-day Mozambique).

Prester John
Travellers told tales of Prester ('priest') John, a rich ruler. He was first said to be a Christian king in Asia, and later to be ruler of Ethiopia in Africa. He was said to have a magic mirror in which he saw everything going on in his empire.

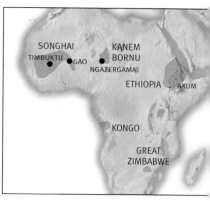

△ This map shows the most important kingdoms of Africa at this time – Songhai in the western sub-Sahara region, Kanem-Bornu further east, Ethiopia in the mountainous northwest, and Great Zimbabwe in central-southern Africa.

TOKUGAWA JAPAN

The Tokugawa, or Edo, period in Japan marked the end of a series of civil wars and fighting amongst Warlords for control of the country. Tokugawa Ieyasu became the first of the Tokugawa shoguns (powerful military leaders and effective rulers of Japan) in 1603. He and his descendants presided over a long period of stability.

Ieyasu governed from the village of Edo, which became a huge, fortified town (now Tokyo). He reorganized the country into regions called domains, each of which was led by a daimyo. Each daimyo controlled local groups of warriors, known as samurai, and promised to support Ieyasu as shogun. This helped bring peace to Japan.

At first, Japan was open to foreigners and often visited by Portuguese, English and Dutch traders. Tokugawa shoguns feared that Christianity might undermine their ability to rule and all foreigners were banned from 1637. Despite Japan's isolation, the country flourished. Population and food production increased, but taxes were heavy and many small crimes were punishable by death.

Eventually, rebellions started which led to the Tokugawa Dynasty being overthrown in 1867.

Under the Tokugawas, society was rigidly controlled – people were expected to commit suicide if they were disgraced. Wealthy women were treated as ornaments. They had to wear very high shoes and long gowns, which made it almost impossible for them to walk, while complicated hairstyles made it difficult for them to move their heads.

▽ *Samurai warriors were trained to fight from childhood. Their main weapons were bows and arrows, single-edged swords and daggers. They fought on foot or on horseback and wore armour and masks to make them look more frightening as well as for protection.*

◁ *Tokugawa Ieyasu (1543–1616) as shogun encouraged agriculture and Confucianism in Japan. He firmly controlled the nobles and their families.*

COLONIZING NORTH AMERICA

The Spanish and French were the first Europeans to explore North America. French traders and missionaries explored the north, which they named Canada, while to the south, the Spanish founded what is now New Mexico, exploring California and Texas.

In the late 16th century, small groups of Europeans began to settle in North America.

Many early colonies failed but an English explorer, Sir Walter Raleigh, set up a successful colony named Jamestown. Although the colonists had to struggle against hunger, disease and battles with the Native Americans, whose land they were occupying, the colony managed to survive, encouraging other people to join them.

Famous early settlers, the Pilgrim Fathers, were religious dissenters looking for a place to practise their religion in peace. Leaving Plymouth, England, in 1620 they eventually landed near Cape Cod in Massachusetts.

Like many of the first settlers, they relied heavily on help from and trade with the Native Americans to survive. Four years later, the Dutch West India Company founded the colony of New Netherlands on the Hudson River and in 1625 they built a trading post on Manhattan Island, calling it New Amsterdam.

Meanwhile the French were starting to colonize Canada. Samuel de Champlain founded Quebec in 1608 and from there he explored beyond the St Lawrence River as far as Lake Huron, claiming all the land for France. Later, other French explorers in the south travelled along the Mississippi River and claimed the whole river valley for France, calling it Louisiana after the French king Louis XIV.

Many of the colonists earned their living by farming, producing food for themselves and crops for export to Europe, such as tobacco, indigo and rice. There were also many traders and trappers who either exchanged European goods, such as guns and alcohol, with the Native Americans for animal furs, or hunted and trapped the animals for themselves.

◁ *Many Native Americans helped early settlers to survive. They taught them which crops were best suited to the land and climate and how to raise them. They also traded goods with the settlers.*

Europeans fight for North America
The English, French and Spanish claimed large areas of North America, even though large populations of Native Americans lived there. Some settlers tried to convert the Native Americans to Christianity. Others came to trade, especially in furs, or to farm. As colonization increased, bitter battles were fought over the land.

◁ *The first settlements were built near a good water supply. Settlers cut down trees to build simple log cabins and barns for their animals. The cleared land was fenced in and used for growing crops such as maize and squash. Turkeys were kept for food and tobacco was grown for export.*

71

THE SLAVE TRADE

Africa had a long history of slavery, but until the early 16th century this was only on a relatively small scale. This changed when Europeans started to visit the African coasts.

European colonies in America and the Caribbean required much manpower to work on plantations. Native peoples were often enslaved but bad conditions and European diseases wiped out large numbers. The search for more workers led to Europeans heading into the African interior. Chained together, African slaves were forced to endure terrible conditions onboard ships with little light, air, food or water. As many as a third died on each eight-week journey.

Those that survived were frequently split from their families, sold at auction and put to heavy work on farms and plantations. Life was terribly hard; they were often badly fed and frequently beaten for the smallest mistake. Many died quickly and few survived more than ten years.

The slave trade reached its peak in the 18th century, with over six million Africans shipped to America. Many traditional African societies were devastated while others grew rich on the trade and rose to power.

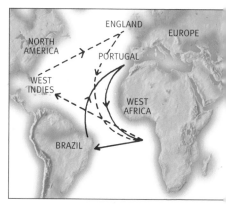

△ This map shows the triangular trade route taken by slave ships. Ships sailed from Europe to Africa with guns and cloth to buy slaves. They then went on to the Americas where the slaves were sold before returning home with sugar, rum and cotton.

◁ Slave ships were designed to carry more than 400 people, packed in as tightly as possible, on the two month voyage from West Africa to the Americas.

◁ Slaves were often brutally ill-treated. This slave is wearing a heavy iron collar to prevent him lying down to make sure that he could not rest while he was working. Many slaves were worked to death.

THE ENGLISH CIVIL WAR

King Charles I came to the throne in 1625 and, after many clashes with the House of Commons, he dissolved parliament in 1629. He recalled parliament in 1640 after a rebellion had broken out in Scotland. Again he clashed with parliament and when he tried to arrest leading members, civil war became inevitable.

◁ *Parliament's soldiers were known as Roundheads because of their short hair cuts. They wore iron breastplates and helmets.*

▷ *Royalist soldiers were also called Cavaliers. They wore their hair long and dressed flamboyantly. Most Royalists were Catholics or members of the aristocracy.*

With the first major battle in 1642 leading to no clear victor, the next four years saw fighting take place all over the country. Towns and families were divided in their support with rich and poor on both sides. Parliament's forces, led by able generals such as Oliver Cromwell, eventually defeated the royalists in 1645. Charles managed to escape and plotted a second civil war which broke out in 1648 but was quickly crushed. He was executed in 1649 and for 11 years, England became a republic. The people wanted a king once more so, in 1660, Charles's son was invited back from exile to reign as Charles II.

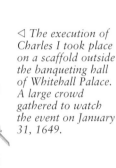

◁ *The execution of Charles I took place on a scaffold outside the banqueting hall of Whitehall Palace. A large crowd gathered to watch the event on January 31, 1649.*

LOUIS XIV

Louis XIV of France reigned for 72 years. He was an absolute ruler who made decisions without regard to the common people or the nobility. Early on in his reign, disagreements with the council of nobles and a peoples' rebellion against heavy taxes caused Louis to dismiss the council and rule with his own hand-picked advisers.

His chief adviser was Jean Colbert, controller-general of finance. France was already the most powerful country in Europe and Colbert's policies: reorganizing taxes, reforming the legal system, improving communications and building new industries and a powerful navy, made it the most efficient, too. Louis spent much of France's wealth on extravagances such as the magnificent palace at Versailles and also on wars to expand France's boundaries. But the ordinary people paid a heavy price with high taxes, the persecution of French Protestants and no help when bad harvests led to thousands starving to death. When Louis died in 1715, France was left financially weak.

△ The magnificent palace of Versailles, 18km southwest of Paris, was the centre of government.

◁ Louis XIV (1638–1715) was glorified by artists and writers as the Sun King. He was protective of his personal reputation, which he considered to be inseparable from that of France.

The plays of Molière
One of Louis XIV's favourite dramatists was Jean Baptiste Molière (1622–1673), often called the father of modern French comedy.

REVOLUTION & INDUSTRY

The period 1700-1900 was a time of conflict, revolution and great political, economic and social change. Revolutions in agriculture, industry and transport made travel easier and increasingly concentrated people in towns where factory work replaced traditional rural existence.

To find raw materials and markets for factory goods, many European countries began to build up new empires overseas. Britain claimed Australia, New Zealand and much of the Pacific, while there was a scramble between European powers for Africa.

The 13 American colonies declared their independence from Britain in 1776 to become the United States of America. They were helped by the French, who in 1789 had their own revolution, over-throwing their king. Wars in Europe between France and many other countries ended in 1815 with the defeat of Napoleon. Later conflicts in Europe united the separate states of Germany and Italy into the two countries.

China, Japan and Russia stayed largely isolated from the rest of the world and gradually stagnated. Millions of Europeans settled in the United States of America, forcing Native Americans to leave their lands. Conflict over slavery in the USA led to a four-year civil war.

PETER THE GREAT

When Peter the Great came to power at the end of the 17th century, Russia had already been expanding but was still isolated and backward compared to the rest of Europe. Peter was determined to change this and for 18 months toured western Europe learning from kings, scientists and industrial workers. He returned to Russia intent on putting his new knowledge to good use. He encouraged new industries and farming, improved the army and built new roads and canals to help trade. When Peter died in 1725, Russia was more secure and advanced, but life for peasants in the countryside had worsened as taxes increased.

Nearly 40 years after his death, Catherine the Great carried on Peter's ambition. Like Peter I, she encouraged western ideas and used warfare to gain territory for Russia, fighting Sweden and the Ottoman Empire. She was feared by many European leaders but life for the ordinary people of Russia remained very tough.

△ A carriage with runners, like a sleigh, gliding through the snow. Russian winters were so cold and snowy that carriage wheels had to be removed and replaced by runners.

▷ Peter the Great ruled Russia from 1682 to 1725. An immensely tall (over 2m) and strong man, his physical presence matched his character. Energetic and strong-willed he could be brutal, even imprisoning and torturing his own son.

Boyars
The boyars were a group of wealthy landowners who advised the Russian rulers. After his visit to Europe, Peter the Great abolished the boyars' powers and cut off their beards as a visible sign of the great changes that were sweeping Russia.

MANCHU CHINA

The Ming Dynasty had ruled China since 1368, but in the early 17th century, rebellions against high taxes and an unpopular government began. Tribes in Manchuria, northeast of China, united and took advantage of the unrest to seize control and establish the Qing Dynasty which ruled for more than 250 years.

The Manchus considered themselves superior to the Chinese and lived apart from them.

They did, however, adopt the Chinese way of government and gradually adopted the Chinese way of life. Under the Qing Dynasty, China flourished once more. Its empire and population tripled in size. China was basically capable of feeding all of its people and grew tea for export as well as trading silk, porcelain and cotton with Europeans. For many years the Chinese would only accept gold and silver in trade as they believed their products were superior to the Europeans. Despite European pressure to open trade, Chinese emperors resisted, wanting to keep China isolated. This policy gradually changed China from a successful country to a backward one.

◁ Only the emperor was allowed to wear a silk gown embroidered with a five-clawed dragon. On taking control of China, the Manchu made the Chinese wear their hair in a pigtail as a sign of loyalty.

△ This map shows the size of the Qing Dynasty's empire in orange. It is much larger than China today – shown in blue.

77

THE ENLIGHTENMENT

The Enlightenment was a period from the late 17th century into the 18th century, when new ideas about government, personal freedom and religious beliefs began to develop in Europe.

The Enlightenment was influenced by the growth in scientific knowledge that began in the mid-17th century. People looked for reasons why things happened as they did. Modern chemistry and biology grew out of this questioning and our knowledge of physics and astronomy increased greatly. Medicine also improved as people began to study the human body and how it worked.

During the 18th century people began to look at the whole world and the role of people within it. The French philosopher and writer François Marie Voltaire attacked the Church and governments of the day. Another Frenchman, Jean-Jacques Rousseau, criticized civilization itself, saying people should not try to obtain more possessions or power than they needed. Both challenged the idea of absolute monarchy and the tradition that the nobility and clergy were entitled to special privileges. Other great thinkers of the Enlightenment included the economist Adam Smith, the historian David Hume, the philosopher Immanuel Kant, and the writers Mary Wollstonecraft and Samuel Johnson.

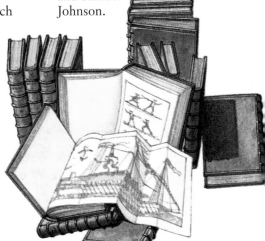

▷ *The Encyclopédie, compiled by Frenchman Denis Diderot, was written by experts in many different subjects and aimed to further all branches of knowledge. The first of the eventual 17 volumes of text and 11 volumes of pictures was published in 1751.*

◁ François Marie Voltaire (1694–1778), novelist, playwright, scientist and philosopher. He famously said, "I may disagree with what you say, but I will defend to the death your right to say it."

◁ A botanical drawing of sunflowers from Philosophia Botanica by Carl Linnaeus, published in 1751. Linneaus was a Swedish botanist who was the first to classify the plant and animal kingdoms.

These new ideas, together with those of other scholars and philosophers of the time, spread rapidly. Many had their thoughts published in books or pamphlets. Others wrote letters to the newspapers or gave lectures. The wealthy and well educated in France often met in the drawing-rooms of noblewomen to discuss the latest books, plays and issues of the day. People began to question the way they were governed. A belief that everyone had the right to knowledge, freedom and happiness inspired the American War of Independence and the French Revolution and eventually led to an end to slavery and the break up of Spain's empire in South America.

Influential women

The scene below shows a lecture being given in the salon of Madame Geoffrin in Paris, in 1725. Noblewomen like Madame Geoffrin were great patrons of learning and the arts. By persuading well-known scholars, writers and philosophers to give private lectures in their homes, they encouraged the discussion of new ideas. Women such as Marie Anne Lavoisier also helped advance science. She assisted her husband, Antoine Lavoisier, in his experiments on gas and later edited his work.

BIRTH of the USA

Before 1750, fighting frequently broke out between British and French colonists in North America over trade and wars in Europe. This fighting was brought to an end when British control of all Canada was agreed by the signing of the Treaty of Paris at the end of the Seven Years War (1756–1763).

With the threat from the French removed, British colonists in America no longer relied on Britain for defence. But Britain needed American taxes to pay for governing their new French territories. By this time there were about two million people living in Britain's 13 colonies in America. They produced most of the food and goods they needed, but taxes were imposed on imported goods, such as tea, and legal documents.

By 1770 the colonists were becoming increasingly unhappy with the British government. Even though they had to pay British taxes they had no say in how government was run. The colonists declared that 'taxation without representation is tyranny'. Britain reacted by sending more soldiers and, in April 1775, an armed confrontation between colonists and British troops took place at Lexington in Massachusetts. The colonists formed an army of their own, commanded by George Washington and on June 17 the two armies clashed at Bunker Hill, near Boston. The British were

Paul Revere
Paul Revere is one of the heroes of the War of Independence. He rode from Boston to Lexington to warn of the approach of British soldiers. Although he was captured, his mission was successful.

successful, but the War of Independence had begun.

Fighting continued and on July 4, 1776 the colonial leaders passed the Declaration of Independence from Britain. The British government refused to accept this. Under Washington's continuing command, the colonists' army increased in size, becoming better equipped and better trained, and began defeating the British. France, Spain and the Netherlands all joined in on the colonists' side, making it difficult for Britain to keep its army supplied. The six-year war ended in 1781 when the British surrendered at Yorktown. Two years later, Britain recognized an independent United States of America.

◁ British troops, trained for fighting in European wars, found fighting in America very different. Standing in close-packed ranks, firing volleys of shot, they presented good targets for the American sharpshooters. The British won the battle of Bunker Hill (1775), but at a terrible cost of 1,000 casualties against 400 American casualties.

▷ British infantrymen wore red long-tailed coats and so were known as 'redcoats'.

81

FRANCE AND NAPOLEON

In the late 18th century, class conflict in France reached a head after poor harvests, higher taxes and knowledge of the Enlightenment and the American War of Independence had created unrest. Louis XVI, king of France, was eventually deposed and after still refusing to give power to the people, he was executed in Paris in 1793. There followed an unruly period called the Reign of Terror during which thousands were arrested and executed.

With the threat of further civil war and with war declared on France by a number of European powers, a new government, the Directoire, was set up which ruled until 1799.

During this period, a brilliant army general, Napoleon Bonaparte, was successfully winning campaigns both inside and outside of France. Born in Corsica, Napoleon defended Paris against rebels in 1796 and conquered a number of Italian states before conducting a campaign in Egypt.

France needed strong leadership after the instability following the Revolution and many welcomed Napoleon's return to France. In 1802 he became First Consul and two years later, Emperor of France. He reorganized France, and in 1804 introduced the Code Napoleon which protected property rights, established the equality of all people before the law and allowed people to practise their religion freely.

As well as ruling France, Napoleon continued leading its army. He was a brilliant general and had thousands of conscripted men at his command. He fought for control of the seas but a combined French and Spanish fleet were defeated at Trafalgar in 1805.

By 1812, Napoleon had control of a vast area of Europe. He seemed undefeatable until a disastrous attempted invasion of Russia failed and his army in Spain and Portugal suffered setbacks. By 1813 Napoleon's empire was collapsing and in 1814 he was forced to abdicate. But he returned with a new army which defeated the Prussians before being beaten at Waterloo. Napoleon was exiled to St Helena.

▽ *Napoleon, as well as being commander of the French army, was also admiral of the French navy, in whose uniform he is shown here. In 1806, he tried to disrupt British trade by using his ships to blockade all ports under French control, but this was not successful.*

▷ *A cartoon of the Duke of Wellington who was given a dukedom in 1814 after defeating Napoleon's armies in Spain. In 1815, Wellington defeated Napoleon again, at Waterloo.*

◁ *During the Reign of Terror around 500,000 people were arrested and 17,000 of them were put to death by public execution on the guillotine. Many of the victims were aristocrats, whose deaths attracted large crowds. Their bodies were buried in unmarked graves.*

THE INDUSTRIAL REVOLUTION

The Industrial Revolution began in Britain in the mid-18th century, transforming society as people moved from the countryside to the town in order to work in factories. Two events in the early 18th century helped make the Industrial Revolution possible. The first was Abraham Darby's discovery that coke instead of charcoal was a better fuel for smelting iron. The second was Thomas Newcomen's improved steam engine, used to pump water out of coal mines. These two inventions meant that more coal and better quality iron could be produced for industry.

Until the 1760s most goods were hand-made by people working at home or in small workshops. Many were spinners and weavers, producing woollen or linen cloth. From the start of the century, however, there had been a rising demand for cotton cloth for clothes. At first cotton was imported from India as rolls of ready-made cloth, but then raw cotton was imported and British spinners and weavers started manufacturing the cloth themselves.

In 1733 the invention of a flying shuttle speeded up the weaving process so much that ordinary spinning wheels could not produce enough yarn.

Inventions such as the Spinning Jenny and Richard Arkwright's

◁ Children worked in coal mines from the age of five. Older children pulled heavy loads from the coal face to the bottom of the shaft, while younger children sat all day in total darkness, opening and closing doors to let the air circulate.

△ *A pithead at Liverpool in England painted in 1792. In the centre is a steam pump used to drain water from the mine. Steam engines were used to power all kinds of machinery in factories and mines.*

spinning frame increased yarn production and the cotton industry began to develop on a very large scale. By 1790, James Watt's improvements to the steam engine meant that steam power could be used to drive machinery. This also increased the demand for coal to heat the water to make steam and for iron to make the engines and other machinery. Coal mines became bigger and deeper and iron works and foundries expanded, while canals (and later railways) were built to bring raw materials to the factories and take the finished goods away.

Towns boomed as people moved in to be near their place of work. Both housing and working conditions were often poor and many people, including children, suffered from malnutrition, disease, or accidents at work.

Spinning Jenny

James Hargreaves, inventor of the Spinning Jenny, was a poor spinner and weaver. He named his new machine after his daughter, Jenny. Other hand-spinners feared the machine would put them out of work, and broke into Hargreaves' house and destroyed his machines, forcing him to move to another town.

85

EUROPE in TURMOIL

At the end of the Napoleonic Wars, much of Europe was in a state of chaos. Many people were living in poverty as a result of the wars and because the population of Europe had almost doubled in just a century. Few ordinary people had the right to vote so the only way they could bring about change was by revolution.

Revolt broke out in France in 1830 and quickly spread to other countries as a growing number of people read about events in newspapers. These were crushed but were followed by mass uprisings throughout Europe in 1848, fuelled by poverty, desire for political reform and in some cases, national independence or unification. Although these uprisings were quashed, the ideas that drove them remained. Many governments started to make reforms while philosophers, scholars and economists looked for different ways of governing and distributing wealth more fairly. The Communist Manifesto published in 1848 by German socialists Karl Marx and Friedrich Engels was particularly influential.

▽ *The revolutions of 1848 were set off by a small revolt in Palermo, Sicily on January 20.*

Feargus O'Connor

Feargus O'Connor (1794–1855) was elected to the British Parliament in 1832 as member for County Cork in Ireland. He lost his seat in 1835 and began agitating for votes for all men. He led the Chartists from 1841 until 1848 and was known for brilliant speeches.

SOUTH AMERICAN INDEPENDENCE

By 1800 Spain and Portugal still ruled vast colonies in South America. Most colonists hated being ruled by foreigners and had fought unsuccessfully for independence. As the Napoleonic Wars in Europe brought chaos to Spain and Portugal, the colonies decided to try to set themselves free again.

◁ At the battle of Ayachucho in 1824, Simón Bolívar's army defeated the Spanish, finally securing independence for Peru.

▷ José de San Martin freed Argentina from Spanish rule, then led his army over the Andes Mountains to help the people of Chile gain their independence, too.

The main fight against Spanish rule was led by Simón Bolívar from Venezuela and José de San Martin from Argentina. San Martin gained freedom for his country in 1816, but Simón Bolívar's fight was longer. He had joined a rebel army which had had some success and became its leader in 1811. Realizing he could not defeat the Spanish in open battle, he led his army over the Andes in a surprise attack in 1819. Two years later, he freed Venezuela and in 1822 he freed Ecuador and Panama from Spanish rule. He then made them all part of a new state, called the Republic of Gran Colombia, with himself as president. Finally Peru was liberated and part of it was renamed Bolivia after Bolívar.

87

THE AMERICAN CIVIL WAR

In the United States, by the early 19th century, the northern and southern states had slowly drifted apart for economic and social reasons. In the North, industry and trade had developed. In the South, however, there was little industry and vast plantations relied greatly on slave labour to grow cotton for export.

In the North, slavery had been banned since 1820, and when Abraham Lincoln was elected president in 1861, his party planned to outlaw slavery completely. Many people in the South saw this as a threat to their way of life and, in 1861, 11 southern states announced that they were breaking away from the Union to form their own Confederacy. When the United States government told them they had no right to do this, civil war broke out.

The other 23 states remained in the Union, so the North had more soldiers and more money, as well as the industry to provide the weapons and supplies they needed for war.

The North also controlled the navy and so was able to blockade southern ports, cutting off trade and wealth. In spite of this, the early battles of the war were won by the South, which had brilliant generals and great enthusiasm for the fight. In July 1863, however, the war turned in favour of the

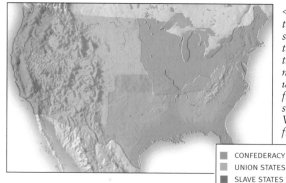

◁ This map shows the 11 Confederate states that broke from the Union. The Union then comprised the north-eastern and west-coast states and five northerly slave states, including West Virginia, which split from Virginia.

■ CONFEDERACY
■ UNION STATES
■ SLAVE STATES WHICH DID NOT SECEDE
■ BREAKAWAY STATE (WEST VIRGINIA)
■ TERRITORIES

North when Unionist troops won the battle of Gettysburg, Pennsylvania, and another Unionist army captured the Confederate town of Vicksburg, Mississippi. In this same year Lincoln announced the complete abolition of slavery which was later approved by Congress in 1865.

The war continued until April 1865 when the Confederate general Robert E Lee surrendered at Appomattox, Virginia. By this time, much of the South was in ruins. On both sides thousands of people had died in battle but also due to disease and hunger. Five days after the surrender, Lincoln was shot by an assassin. Though the war was over, much bitterness remained in the South.

General Robert E Lee
Robert Edward Lee (1807–1870) was born in Virginia. Towards the end of the War he became commander of the Confederate forces. Although his side lost, he was an outstanding leader.

▽ *At the battle of Bull Run, Virginia, 1861, Confederate forces (right) under generals 'Stonewall' Jackson and Beauregard defeated the Union army (left). It was the first major battle of the Civil War.*

NEW NATIONS

After 1815, Italy was composed of a number of states run by foreign powers, particularly Austria. During the 1820s and 30s opposition to foreign rule grew. Revolutions broke out in many states in 1848. These were crushed but were followed by more successful revolts. One state, Piedmont-Sardinia, allied itself with France to defeat Austria, and in 1861, Italy was declared a kingdom. Venice and Rome became part of Italy in 1866 and 1871 respectively.

Germany, like Italy, was also composed of many separate states. In 1815, 38 states formed the German Confederation with Austria and Prussia the most powerful. These two competed for control and in 1866, Prussia declared war on Austria. The victorious Prussians divided the German Confederation, creating a separate North German Confederation which they dominated. War between France and Prussia lasted ten months with France losing Alsace and Lorraine in 1871. The same year saw the German Second Empire declared with William II, King of Prussia, as its emperor and Otto von Bismarck as its chancellor.

◁ *Otto von Bismarck (1815–1898) became Prussian foreign minister in 1862. He was determined to unite the north German states and make Prussia the ruler of a united Germany. To achieve this, he went to war with Austria and France. Germany was finally united in 1871 and Bismarck became its first chancellor.*

▷ *The revolutionary, Giuseppe Garibaldi handing the Kingdom of the Two Sicilies to Victor Emmanuel in 1860. Victor Emmanuel was proclaimed the first king of a united Italy in 1861.*

THE SCRAMBLE
FOR AFRICA

In 1880 less than five percent of Africa was ruled by European powers. But within 20 years the situation had changed completely in what is known as the Scramble for Africa.

Seven European nations, Belgium, Britain, France, Spain and the newly-unified nations of Italy and Germany, took control of almost the whole continent. They were aided by advances in medicine and transport and by the opening of the Suez Canal. This linked the Mediterranean to the Red Sea and greatly reduced journey lengths to East Africa and India.

In 1884, the seven European powers met in Berlin to divide Africa up peacefully between themselves. This was done with no regard for the African peoples, their cultures or any natural boundaries. Any resistance was crushed by large, well-equipped European armies. Many thousands died fighting and many more suffered great hardship as their traditional ways of life were destroyed and they were forced to work as cheap labour in mines and on cotton, tea, coffee and cocoa plantations.

△ This map shows Africa in 1914, when the European powers had colonies there. Only two countries in Africa remained independent: Ethiopia and Liberia.

▽ Patriotic posters appeared in Britain during the Boer Wars (1899–1902). Around 20,000 Boer women and children died in British concentration camps in South Africa.

▷ Cecil Rhodes (1853–1902) was born in Britain, moved to Africa at the age of 17 and eventually became prime minister of the Cape Colony in 1890. He helped bring more territory under British control, but he failed in his ambition to give Britain an empire in Africa that stretched from the Cape to Egypt.

VOTES FOR WOMEN

During the 19th century, political reforms in many European countries started to give ordinary men a vote or a say in how their country was run, but not women.

A movement promoting women's suffrage (the right to vote) began in the United States and gained in strength, inspiring women in other countries. In 1893 New Zealand became the first country to allow women to vote in national elections. In 1903, Emmeline Pankhurst set up a society in Britain called the Women's Social and Political Union (WSPU). It believed in actions rather than words and the WSPU held public demonstrations and attacked property in protest against women's lack of rights. Many of its members were arrested and sent to prison.

With the outbreak of World War I, many women took on and succeeded at jobs traditionally done by men. In 1918 the vote was given to all British women over 30 (it was lowered to 21 in 1928). Adult women in the US were given the right to vote in 1920.

▷ *Emmeline Pankhurst, founder of the WSPU, was arrested and imprisoned several times for destroying property. Other tactics included non-payment of taxes and disrupting political meetings.*

▽ *Many women campaigned peacefully for the right to vote. Known as suffragists (to distinguish them from the more militant suffragettes), they marched and held rallies to gain support.*

THE MODERN WORLD

The 20th century has seen massive and rapid change. At its start, large areas of the world were still controlled by European powers. Two World Wars, the Great Depression, rebellions, revolutions and fights for independence changed the world and the way it was ruled.

The end of World War II (1939-45) saw the European empires finally broken up with many of their colonies granted independence. The US and the Soviet Union emerged as superpowers, while Europe was divided between the capitalist West, supported by the US, and the communist East, supported by the Soviets. Communists also came to power in China. The two superpowers fought a Cold War with both seeking to extend their world influence and competing in an arms race, although direct war was avoided. The Cold War abruptly ended with the collapse of the Soviet Union in 1991. The world today is much smaller and changes faster than ever before.

WORLD WAR I

Towards the end of the 19th century, there was growing rivalry among the nations of Europe. Germany was quickly becoming a major industrial and military power and many countries, especially France and Britain, felt threatened by this. At the same time, Turkey's Ottoman Empire was breaking up. Newly-independent Serbia was gaining power and the empire of Austria-Hungary saw this as a threat. Several great alliances were formed between nations. By 1914 it only needed one incident to spark off a war. This came when the heir to the throne of Austria-Hungary, Archduke Franz Ferdinand, was assassinated by a Serbian.

▽ In the trenches soldiers on both sides were comparatively safe. There they ate and slept, while waiting for orders to go into battle. Dugouts, or underground shelters, offered some protection from enemy shells and the worst of the rain, but the trenches were usually cold, muddy and wet.

Austria-Hungary declared war on Serbia, prompting Russia to mobilize its army to defend Serbia. Germany declared war on Russia and on France, Russia's ally. The following day the German army marched through Belgium to attack France. This drew Britain

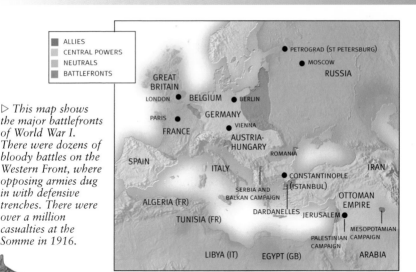

▷ *This map shows the major battlefronts of World War I. There were dozens of bloody battles on the Western Front, where opposing armies dug in with defensive trenches. There were over a million casualties at the Somme in 1916.*

- ALLIES
- CENTRAL POWERS
- NEUTRALS
- BATTLEFRONTS

GREAT BRITAIN
LONDON
PARIS
FRANCE
SPAIN
ALGERIA (FR)
TUNISIA (FR)
LIBYA (IT)
BELGIUM
BERLIN
GERMANY
VIENNA
AUSTRIA-HUNGARY
ITALY
ROMANIA
SERBIA AND BALKAN CAMPAIGN
PETROGRAD (ST PETERSBURG)
MOSCOW
RUSSIA
IRAN
CONSTANTINOPLE (ISTANBUL)
OTTOMAN EMPIRE
DARDANELLES
JERUSALEM
PALESTINIAN CAMPAIGN
MESOPOTAMIAN CAMPAIGN
ARABIA
EGYPT (GB)

into the war. Known as the Great War or World War I, it eventually involved many of the countries of the world.

They were divided into two groups, known as the Allies and the Central Powers. The Central Powers were made up of Germany, Austria-Hungary and Turkey, while the Allies included France, Britain and its empire, Russia, Italy, Japan and, from 1917, the United States.

The war was fought along two main lines, or fronts: the Western Front, which ran from Belgium, through France to Switzerland, and the Eastern Front which ran from the Baltic to the Black Sea. There was also fighting in the Middle East and along the border between Italy and Austria.

In a war of horrific casualties, stalemate existed between the two sides for much of the war. The arrival of over a million troops from the United States by the middle of 1918 was a key turning point. A defeated Germany signed an armistice with the allied forces on the November 11, 1918, bringing the war to an end.

World War I Planes
World War I (1914–1918) was the first war in which aeroplanes were widely used. Flimsy and unreliable, they were first used to spy on enemy trenches and troop movements; later, in aerial combat and in bombing raids. Two of the most famous aeroplanes were the British Sopwith Camel, which was a biplane (which means it had two pairs of wings), and the German Fokker E1, which was a monoplane (one pair of wings).

SOPWITH CAMEL

GERMAN FOKKER

THE RUSSIAN REVOLUTION

Tsar Alexander II realized his country was very backward compared with the rest of Europe. He attempted many modernizations and reforms including freeing serfs, improving government, education and encouraging the development of industry and the railways. Many people, however, thought his reforms did not go far enough and in 1881 he was assassinated. His successor, Alexander III, promptly undid most of the reforms. Unrest began to grow and people such as Vladimir Lenin looked to the writings of Karl Marx, the founder of communism, for ways of changing Russian life. The first serious rebellion broke out in 1905 after troops fired on striking workers in the capital, St Petersburg. It was soon crushed and the leaders, including Lenin, went into exile.

△ Tsar Nicholas II with his wife Alexandra and their five children. After the revolution, they were all imprisoned. In 1918 they were executed.

When World War I started, life for most people in Russia went from bad to worse. The economy almost collapsed and people started to go hungry. The government did nothing to improve the situation and in March 1917 riots broke out again. This time the troops joined the rioters. Tsar Nicholas II resigned and a temporary government was set up but unrest continued. The Bolsheviks, led by Lenin, attacked the Winter Palace in St Petersburg and seized power, an event known as the October Revolution.

The new government led by Lenin moved the capital to Moscow and made peace with Germany. It broke up the landowner large estates and gave the land to the peasants who worked on it. The workers took control of the factories and the state took control of the banks. Not everyone agreed with this, however, and in 1918 civil war broke out between the Bolshevik Red Army and the anti-communist White Russians. This ended in victory for the Bolsheviks in 1921. The following year, the Union of Soviet Socialist Republics was formed. After Lenin's death in 1924, he was succeeded by Joseph Stalin. Stalin's rule was oppressive and many of his opponents were killed.

△ Vladimir Ilyich Lenin (1870–1924), a lawyer, was exiled to Siberia in 1897 for his political views. He became leader of the Bolsheviks who wanted major reforms in the way Russia was governed. He was exiled again from January 1905 to March 1917, but on his return to Russia his strong personality and powerful speeches persuaded thousands of ordinary people to join the revolution.

▽ Armed workers led by the Bolsheviks stormed St Petersburg's Winter Palace in 1917, starting the revolution. They were joined by Russian soldiers, tired of fighting the Germans in World War I.

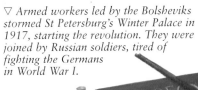

THE GREAT DEPRESSION

After World War I, the economies of many European countries were in chaos. Germany had to pay reparations (large sums of money) to Britain and France for starting the war. This led its economy to collapse in the 1920s. Other nations also suffered as they tried to pay back money borrowed to finance their war effort.

Most of the money borrowed to finance the war came from the United States. There, many people had invested in stocks and shares, pushing their prices up beyond their real value. Share prices reached a peak in August 1929, then started to dip. Investors panicked and started to sell recklessly. Prices fell and fell and thousands lost all their money. This is called the Wall Street Crash and started an economic crisis as many banks and businesses closed down. The situation was made worse as a severe drought hit the agricultural states of the Midwest and, combined with years of over-farming, created the enormous Dust Bowl in which nothing would grow. Many farms were abandoned.

The economic crisis in the US soon affected the whole world. As loans were called in by the US, economies came close to collapsing. This brought severe economic problems to Europe, especially Britain and Germany, both of which had high unemployment. At the height of the Depression in 1932,

△ Unemployment figures rose throughout the world during the Great Depression. The worst hit countries were the USA, Britain and Germany, whose economies were heavily based on industry.

world exports of raw materials had fallen by over 70 per cent, ruining the economies of many colonies who depended on the export of food and raw materials for their income.

The US was particularly badly hit. Mass unemployment led to many being made homeless, reduced to living in shanty towns of tin and cardboard. In 1933, however, a new government led by Franklin D Roosevelt introduced the New Deal. It included financial support for farmers and a construction programme to create more jobs. Banks were more closely regulated and savings better protected. Even so, unemployment remained high throughout the 1930s.

The New Deal
Part of the New Deal introduced by President Roosevelt in 1933 included a programme to create more jobs. There were also welfare (social security) and labour laws to improve working conditions.

▷ *On the Jarrow Crusade 200 men set out in October 1935 from Jarrow in Northern England to London to draw attention to unemployment in their home town. Helped by sympathizers, they marched all the way on foot.*

THE RISE OF FASCISM

Fascism is the name of a political movement that grew up between the wars. Fascist leaders promised strong leadership and were opposed to socialism. They gained massive support by promising to restore national pride and create jobs.

▽ *Neville Chamberlain, Prime Minister of Britain, waving the Munich agreement of 1938. It was signed in an attempt to keep peace in Europe by recognizing Germany's claim to the Sudetenland.*

Italy was the first country to have a Fascist government when Benito Mussolini marched his followers into Rome in October 1922 threatening to overthrow the current government by force. Asked to form a new government, Mussolini quickly turned Italy into a one-party state killing and terrorizing those political parties which did not agree with him. In 1925, he started ruling as a dictator.

At that time, Spain was also ruled by a dictator called Miguel Primo de Rivera but he fell from power in 1930. His son founded

▷ *Hitler addressing a rally at Nuremburg, 1938. Adolf Hitler (1889–1945) was a powerful speaker who knew exactly how to win the support of his audience. He turned Germany into a police state, persecuting his political opponents, trade unionists and Jews, whom he blamed for all Germany's problems.*

the Falangist party made up of Spanish Fascists. Under the leadership of General Francisco Franco, the Falangists overthrew the elected government in Spain in 1936. Civil war broke out in which Franco, supported by Italy and Germany, eventually defeated the Republicans supported by Russia. In 1939 Franco became dictator of Spain.

In Germany, the Nazi party and its leader Adolf Hitler rose to power in 1933. Hitler started a programme of public works to create jobs and built up munitions and the armed forces. He imposed total control on the people, banning other political parties, introducing a secret police and persecuting minorities, especially the Jews. Hitler also wanted to take back lands Germany lost after World War I. These included the Saar area, which he reoccupied in 1935, and the Rhineland, reoccupied in 1936. In 1938,

△ Benito Mussolini (1883–1945) impressed many Italians with his policies at first. After Italy's disastrous efforts in World War II, he was shot while trying to escape.

Hitler sent tanks into Vienna to persuade the Austrians to agree to a union with Germany and also threatened to take over the Sudetenland in Czechoslovakia. To try to keep the peace, the Munich Agreement of September 1938 gave the Sudetenland to Germany. The following March, however, Hitler's troops took over the whole of Czechoslovakia and began to threaten Poland.

WORLD WAR II

World War II started on September 3, 1939, with Britain and France declaring war on Germany after it had sent troops to invade Poland. The war was fought between the Axis powers (Germany, Italy and Japan) and the Allies (Britain, its Commonwealth, France, the United States and the Soviet Union).

German troops invaded Denmark, Norway, Belgium, the Netherlands and France. The tactics the Germans used became known as the Blitzkrieg, which means 'lightning war'. The Germans overcame any opposition quickly by using vast numbers of tanks in surprise attacks followed by bomber planes and, finally, infantry to complete the take-over.

By June 1940, Italy entered the war on Germany's side and with most of Europe fallen, Hitler planned to invade Britain. His airforce attacked London and southeast England in daylight raids trying to crush both morale and the British air force. With fewer planes, the British managed to defeat the Germans.

A new battle front opened in September 1940 when first Italian, then German troops moved into Egypt. Britain's troops, already stationed there to defend the Suez Canal, beat the

△ *Europe by the end of 1941 was almost completely under German control. On the continent, only neutral countries managed to remain free. Axis troops had also expanded into North Africa.*

Italians but were forced back by the Germans. Buoyed up by his successes, Hitler launched an attack on his former ally the Soviet Union in June 1941, invading the country with the help of Finland, Hungary and Romania. By the end of 1941, however, the United States joined the war, following the bombing of its navy at Pearl Harbor in Hawaii, by the Japanese air force.

After initial successes, German troops in both Africa and the Eastern Front started to be repelled. In October and November 1942, a decisive battle at El Alamein, Egypt, was won by allied forces under the command of Field Marshall Montgomery. The Axis armies in Africa surrendered in May 1943. On The Eastern Front, the Germans failed to capture Leningrad (now St Petersburg) despite a three year siege. They also lost a vital battle at Stalingrad (now Volvograd) and were forced off Soviet soil by August 1944.

△ Winston Churchill (1874–1965) was Prime Minister of Britain from 1940 to 1945. His strong leadership and rousing speeches encouraged people through the worst days of the war. Here he is shown making a 'V' for victory sign.

▽ The Battle of Britain was fought in the skies above southeast England from August to October 1940. Although Britain had far fewer planes than the Germans it still managed to win. Over 2,600 planes were shot down in the battle.

THE WAR ENDS

The Allied Invasion of Europe started in June 1944. Within a month over a million troops had landed and started to advance through Beligum and the Netherlands towards Germany. German forces launched a counter-attack but by January 1945 this was defeated and the Allies' advance continued into the German heartland. Bitter fighting continued but with Soviet forces heading towards Berlin from the East as well, the Germans faced defeat. Hitler committed suicide on April 30th and on May 7th the Germans signed a general surrender.

Although the war in Europe was at an end, fighting continued in Asia. In September 1944, US troops began to recapture the Philippines from the Japanese, while a campaign led by the British started to reconquer Burma. An Allied invasion of Japan was planned for late 1945. Before it could be put into operation, an atomic bomb was dropped on Hiroshima in Japan on July 6, 1945. Three days later a second atomic bomb was dropped on Nagasaki. Thousands of people died in the explosions and many thousands more died

▽ The Allied invasion of Normandy began on June 6, 1944 (D-Day). Around 156,000 troops were landed in the largest sea-borne attack ever mounted.

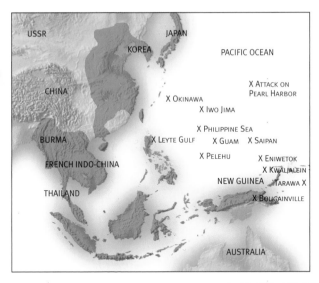

◁ The war in the Pacific began when Japan bombed Pearl Harbor, in 1941. A year later, it held all the orange areas on the map. The crosses mark the ensuing battles.

later from radiation sickness, burns and other injuries. Five days later, the Japanese government under Emperor Hirohito surrendered and on August 14 World War II ended.

Almost six years of fighting had had a devastating effect on the world. The loss of life had been enormous. On both sides there had also been millions of civilian casualties, either through bombing raids or through illness, cold and hunger. Probably the worst affected of all, however, were the Jews of occupied Europe. Hitler had been determined to wipe out the Jewish people and around six million died as a result of slave labour, torture, medical experiments and gassing in concentration camps throughout Germany and Poland. In November 1945, leading Nazis were put on trial at Nuremberg for war crimes and crimes against humanity.

△ The Nuremberg Trials. After World War II, the Allies set up an international military court at Nuremberg in Germany to try the Nazi leaders. Twelve were sentenced to death by hanging and six were sent to prison. Lesser Nazi officials, such as concentration camp commanders, were also tried.

THE COLD WAR

The capitalist United States of America and the communist Soviet Union emerged from World War II as the world's dominant superpowers. Even though they had fought together in World War II, they soon became enemies in what was known as the Cold War.

The Soviet Union set up communist governments in the countries of Eastern Europe. To stop communism spreading to the West, the US-backed Marshall Plan was set up to give financial aid to countries with economies ruined by war.

One of the first conflicts occurred in 1948. After the war Germany was divided between the Allies (US, France, Britain and the Soviet Union). Germany's capital, Berlin, was in Soviet territory but also split amongst the Allies. The Soviets tried to blockade the parts of Berlin held by the other three allied powers but the blockade was defeated by airlifting supplies. Shortly after, Germany was divided into West and East.

Both superpowers distrusted each other and expected an attack at any time. They both formed alliances amongst their allies, NATO in the West and the Warsaw Pact in the East. Both sides also began developing and stockpiling nuclear weapons. This led to another crisis in 1962 when Cuban dictator Fidel Castro

■ NATO COUNTRIES
■ WARSAW PACT
□ NEUTRAL COUNTRIES

FINLAND
RUSSIA
NORWAY
SWEDEN
NETHERLANDS
IRELAND
DENMARK
POLAND
BRITAIN
EAST
BELGIUM WEST GERMANY
GERMANY CZECHOSLOVAKIA
FRANCE AUSTRIA ROMANIA
HUNGARY
PORTUGAL
YUGOSLAVIA
SPAIN SWITZERLAND BULGARIA
ITALY
TURKEY

△ This map shows how Europe was divided after World War II. The boundary between the two halves of Europe was first named the 'iron curtain' by Winston Churchill. Few people were able to cross this divide.

allowed the Soviet Union to build missile bases in Cuba that threatened the USA. President John F Kennedy ordered the US Navy to blockade Cuba and eventually the Soviets agreed to withdraw. Both sides realized the danger of a nuclear war and the missiles were removed.

The USA and the Soviet Union encouraged many countries to take sides in the Cold War and, while they never fought against each other directly, the two superpowers became involved in many armed struggles in all parts of the world. For a time, the two superpowers also competed in space as well. As the Cold War eased, collaboration replaced competition in space with both countries now working together to make further advances.

NATO
The North Atlantic Treaty Organization was set up on April 4, 1949, with its headquarters in Brussels, Belgium. It was a military alliance between several Western European countries, Canada and the United States, against aggression from any outside nation. In 1955, the Soviet Union formed an alliance of communist states, the Warsaw Pact.

▷ Laika the dog was placed on board Sputnik 2 and was the first living creature to go into space. She wore a special suit, but as no one knew how to return the satellite to Earth, she died in space.

◁ The Mir space station was launched by the Soviet Union in 1986. Astronauts from the Soviet Union, the US and other countries have visited Mir to carry out experiments.

DECOLONIZATION

In 1920, Mohandas Karamchand Gandhi become the leader of the Indian National Congress, a political party intent on independence for India. Ghandi launched a lengthy policy of peaceful civil disobedience and non-cooperation with the British which included boycotting British goods. Thousands were arrested, imprisoned and beaten, including Gandhi himself.

The British government agreed to India's independence in 1945. With a sizeable Muslim minority amongst India's Hindu majority, religion was a big problem. The solution imposed in 1947 was for two areas to the north of India to become an independent Muslim country (Pakistan). Millions of people found themselves living in the 'wrong' country – Muslims in India and Hindus in Pakistan – and so mass migrations began. As the people fled, atrocities were inflicted on both sides and hundreds of thousands of people were killed.

△ This map shows how India was divided. East Pakistan became Bangladesh in 1971. Burma (now Myanmar) and Ceylon (Sri Lanka) gained their independence in 1948.

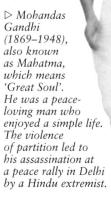

▷ Mohandas Gandhi (1869–1948), also known as Mahatma, which means 'Great Soul'. He was a peace-loving man who enjoyed a simple life. The violence of partition led to his assassination at a peace rally in Delhi by a Hindu extremist.

108

Many African countries gained their independence after World War II. Once they were independent, these countries had to work out and run their own armed forces, economies and systems of government, law and education.

The borders imposed by the European powers in the previous century did not reflect the natural boundaries or ethnic groupings of African people. This led to civil wars in several countries, notably in the Congo, Ethiopia and Nigeria, as people from one area tried to become independent and form a new country of their own. In other countries, such as Angola, Rwanda and Burundi, civil wars broke out between rival ethnic groups, fighting for control.

Problems also occurred in countries where white settlers wanted to stay in control. It was especially difficult in South Africa where, from 1948 to 1990, the

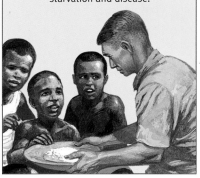

Poverty and famine
Famine has become a great problem in parts of Africa where the land has been over-farmed for too long, the soil is no longer fertile or the rains fail. Conditions are made worse by over-population and civil wars. People have to rely on aid or face starvation and disease.

white government used a system (Apartheid) to keep blacks out of power by not giving them the right to vote. Once Apartheid was abolished, free elections were held and in 1994 Nelson Mandela became the first black president of South Africa.

▷ *Ghanaian chiefs waiting for the first session of parliament. Ghana gained full independence from Britain in 1957.*

WARS IN ASIA

Vietnam, together with Cambodia and Laos, was part of the French colony of Indochina. It was occupied by the Japanese in World War II and during this time the Viet Minh league, led by the communist Ho Chi Minh, declared Vietnam independent.

After the war, France refused to recognize Ho Chi Minh's government and war broke out between the French and Vietnamese. This war ended in defeat for the French at the battle of Dien Bien Phu in 1954. An international agreement then divided Vietnam into communist North and non-communist South.

Almost immediately civil war broke out between the two countries. From 1959, communist guerrillas in the South, known as the Viet Cong, were helped by North Vietnam. The US, worried about the spread of communism, sent military aid to help the South Vietnamese. As the conflict escalated, the US began sending troops to help the South from 1965. The Viet Cong's guerrilla

◁ Most Vietnamese lived by farming, mostly growing rice in the fields around their villages. Many suffered greatly in the war as crops and villages were destroyed to flush out and kill the Viet Cong.

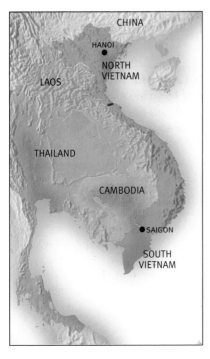

◁ *Most of the war was fought in the jungles of South Vietnam. The Ho Chi Minh trail, from China through Laos into South Vietnam, was the Viet Cong's supply line from the North.*

▽ *US soldiers were expecting to fight a traditional war, with large scale battles between two sides. They had to adapt to the Viet Cong's guerilla tactics using small groups to mount surprise attacks.*

tactics made it very difficult to defeat them. In an attempt to cut off their supply lines, US planes began bombing North Vietnam. At the same time, whole villages in the south and vast areas of forest were sprayed with chemicals to destroy any Viet Cong hiding places.

By 1966, anti-war demonstrations had begun and in 1968, the Viet Cong's major Tet offensive on the South convinced Americans that the war could not be won. In 1969 the US began to withdraw its troops and a cease-fire was agreed in 1973. Fighting continued until 1975, when the North brought the South under its control.

Anti-war Demonstrations
The Vietnam War was the first to be widely covered on television. Once people could see that growing numbers of troops were killed or injured and large parts of Vietnam destroyed, many took to the streets in protest. By 1967, the protests had spread beyond the US and the strength of anti-war feeling helped persuade President Nixon to withdraw from the war.

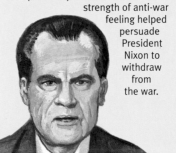

111

THE SOCIAL REVOLUTION

At the start of the second half of the 20th century, many people throughout the world were still treated unequally because of their religion, sex or colour of their skin. Black people were especially discriminated against in education and employment. Many also had to use separate public transport vehicles and public facilities as beaches and lavatories. With few or no civil rights, they could not vote, only protest and campaign, even though this often led to fines, imprisonment or worse.

Many protests occurred in the 1950s in the southern United States over segregation on public buses and at schools and colleges. Many more non-violent protests followed, often inspired by Dr Martin Luther King, a Baptist minister. The largest was a march by 250,000 to Washington, DC, in 1963 to demand equality for all. The following year saw the US government pass the Civil Rights Act, which made discrimination illegal.

Around the same time, the white minority government in South Africa tightened its policy of Apartheid (the separation of whites and blacks). The killing of 69 unarmed protesters in Sharpeville in 1960 saw the formation of a guerrilla army called Umkhonto we Sizwe (Spear of the Nation). One of its most

▷ *Martin Luther King (1929–1968) was an outstanding speaker whose belief in non-violent resistance to oppression won him the Nobel peace prize in 1964. In 1968 he was shot dead in Memphis.*

◁ *Black townships in South Africa were often disturbed by unrest and violence during the 1980s. Many people were killed or injured and vehicles and houses were set alight as a tide of protest arose against Apartheid.*

important members was Nelson Mandela, who in 1963 was imprisoned for life, accused of plotting to overthrow the government. Worldwide protests and sanctions occurred as a result of this action. By 1990 the government, led by F W de Klerk, knew it had to change its policy and Mandela was released from prison. Apartheid was abolished and 1994 saw the first national elections for all adults, no matter their colour.

The struggle for black equality led others to protest against injustice. In the 1960s, women in many countries began to campaign for equal pay and job opportunities, better health care and the right to have abortions. New laws were introduced to ban sex discrimination in employment. In the late 60s, gay men and women also began their long campaign for equal rights.

▽ *Nelson Mandela was born in 1918 and trained as a lawyer. He remained in prison from 1962 until 1990. He was able to vote for the first time in April 1994, when the country held its first free elections. Mandela's party, the ANC, won with a large majority and he became president.*

THE CULTURAL REVOLUTION

When Mao Zedong came to power in China in 1949, many Chinese could not read or write. Many also suffered from ill health and hunger. Mao's government improved health care and provided schools in which adults as well as children could be taught. For the first time, women were given equal rights with men. Large farms were taken from wealthy landowners and divided up among the peasants. New roads and railways and power plants to generate electricity were built. But the problem of providing enough food for everyone remained. In 1958, Mao introduced the Great Leap Forward, to try and make each village self-sufficient, not only by growing its own food, but also by producing its own clothing and tools in small village factories. The plan failed, because the government did not invest enough money in it. Even greater food shortages occurred and many people died of starvation.

In 1959 Mao Zedong retired and his successors tried to solve the economic problems caused by the Great Leap Forward. At the same time, tension grew between China and the Soviet Union. Mao thought the Soviet Union had lost its revolutionary spirit. Not wanting the same to happen to China, he swept back to power in 1966 and launched the Cultural

◁ *This poster of a triumphant Mao appeared in 1949 when he first came to power. He took over a country where many could not read or write and civil war had left the country in financial disorder. Mao's initial reforms, called the Five Year Plan, helped to improve the economy.*

Revolution. Its aim was to overthrow old habits and rid the Communist party and country of people who disagreed with Mao. Young people formed groups of Red Guards who criticized foreigners and their elders. Many artists, writers and teachers were forced to leave their jobs and go to work on the land. Schools, universities, factories and hospitals closed as older members of staff were forced out by students. Many people were killed and others were sent into exile for criticizing Mao.

When Mao died in 1976, the Cultural Revolution came to an end. His successor, Deng Xiaoping, began to open up China to trade and contact with the West.

△ In the Cultural Revolution schools and colleges were closed and teachers and students forced to work on the land. Opposition was brutally put down by the Red Guards.

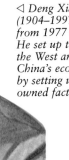

◁ Deng Xiaoping (1904–1997) ruled China from 1977 until his death. He set up trade links with the West and encouraged China's economy to grow by setting up privately owned factories.

115

CRISIS IN THE
MIDDLE EAST

An uneasy peace followed the defeat of the Arab League by Israel in 1948. Jordan had captured Israeli land on the West Bank of the River Jordan, including much of Jerusalem. At the same time, Israel continued to encourage large numbers of Jews to migrate from Europe, Russia and the United States. The Palestinian Arabs were pushed into separate communities within Israel and they began to campaign for a land of their own.

▷ *Saddam Hussein (born 1938) became dictator of Iraq in 1979 and the following year went to war with Iran. In 1990 he launched a war with Kuwait, but was heavily defeated by US-led troops. He managed to keep hold of power, but is deeply distrusted by the West.*

The next crisis came in 1956 when Egypt took control of the Suez Canal. This led to a war, with Egypt on one side and Britain and France, who had previously controlled the canal, on the other. Feeling threatened by this, Israel invaded the Sinai Peninsula and destroyed Egyptian bases there. The third war between Israelis and their Arab neighbours broke out on June 5, 1967 and lasted for six days. In this, Israel destroyed the Egyptian air force and also took control of the whole of Jerusalem, the West Bank, the Golan Heights, the Gaza Strip and Sinai. A fourth war broke out in October 1973 when Egyptian forces attacked Israel across the Suez Canal and Syrian forces attacked on the Golan Heights. Israel managed to defeat both forces.

116

Three years later, fighting broke out in Lebanon, where many Palestinians lived in refugee camps. They joined forces with Lebanese Muslims who were in conflict with Lebanese Christians. Syrian and UN troops were also involved. In 1982, Israel invaded Lebanon to try and drive the Palestinians out, but failed.

From 1980 to 1988 another large-scale war broke out between Iraq and Iran, both of which were major oil-producing countries. Then in 1990 Iraqi troops invaded oil-rich Kuwait. UN forces freed Kuwait in 1991.

Since then, peace agreements have been signed between Israel and Egypt, Jordan and Syria. Israel has granted limited Palestinian self-rule, but tension and conflict continue to disrupt the peace process.

△ This map shows the Middle East in modern times. The shaded areas show land taken by Israel in the Six Day War.

▽ At peace talks in 1993, Israeli prime minister Yitzhak Rabin (left) and Yasser Arafat, leader of the Palestinian Liberation Organization (right) under the guidance of President Clinton (centre), agreed in principle to Palestinian self-rule in Gaza and Jericho.

THE WORLD TODAY

One of the greatest changes in the 20th century has been in the speed at which information can travel around the world. Radio, television and computers along with air travel now make it possible to be in touch and aware of events all over the globe.

One of the biggest concerns of the late 20th century has been for the environment. Pioneering groups, such as Greenpeace and Friends of the Earth, started campaigning in the 1970s over many environmental issues including the destruction of rainforests, endangered species and the dumping of toxic waste. Around the same time, scientists began to study the effects of pollution, especially the increasing amounts of carbon dioxide in the air caused by burning fuels, like coal and oil. Carbon dioxide in the air traps more of the sun's heat leading to global warming. Some progress has been made in environmental protection and reducing carbon dioxide emissions, but there is still a long way to go.

△ Although famine had long been a problem in Africa, television pictures of Ethiopia in 1984 shocked the world. Money poured in to charities to provide food and medicine. This solved the problem in the short term. Now aid agencies realize they must support long-term projects that will help prevent famine in the future.

◁ With the splitting of the Soviet Union, many of the symbols of communist rule, such as this statue of Lenin, were pulled down.

△ In 1969, US astronaut Neil Armstrong became the first person to land on the moon

Politics
c. 3500 BC Sumerians set up city states in Mesopotamia

Politics
c. 1600–1100 BC The Mycenaeans dominate ancient Greece

Politics
147–146 BC Romans invade and conquer Greece

Exploration
c. 3000 BC Phoenician ships sail Mediterranean sea

Exploration
c. 1001 BC People from Southeast Asia begin colonizing Polynesia

Exploration
c. 600 BC Phoenicians sail into Atlantic and possibly round Africa

Technology
c. 3500 BC Sumerians invent writing and the wheel

Technology
c. 2000 BC Babylonians begin counting in 60s – hence 360 in a circle

Technology
c. 500 BC Steel is made in India

Arts
c. 2600 BC Work begins on the Great Pyramid in Egypt

Arts
c. 1100 BC First Chinese dictionary is compiled

Arts
447–438 BC Greeks build the Parthenon temple in Athens

Religion
During this period: Egyptians worship their pharaoh as a god-king

Religion
c. 1500 BC Probable date of the development of the Hindu religion

Religion
c. 563 BC Birth of the Buddha
c. 400 BC The first part of the Bible is finished

Daily Life
c. 8000 BC Farming first practised in Near East and Southeast Asia

Daily Life
c. 1450 BC Volcanic explosion wipes out Cretan civilization

Daily Life
214 BC Building of the Great Wall of China is begun

119

Politics

AD 476 Western Roman Empire collapses
AD 655-698 Arabs dominate North Africa

Politics

1066 King Harold is defeated at Hastings, William of Normandy becomes king

Politics

1206 Tribal chief Temujin is proclaimed Ghengis Khan, ruler of Mongolia

Exploration

AD 399 Chinese monk Fu-Hsien begins journey to India, Sri Lanka and Java

Exploration

1096–1099 The First Crusade goes to Turkey and Palestine

Exploration

1271–1295 Marco Polo spends 24 years at Kublai Khan's court

Technology

AD 150 The Chinese make the first paper

Technology

AD 940 Astronomers in China produce a star map

Technology

c.1290 Cable bridges are built over deep valleys in the Andes

Arts

AD 650 Neumes, early form of music notation, are developed

Arts

AD 942 Arabs introduce trumpets and kettledrums into Europe

Arts

c.1220 Italian poets develop the form of the sonnet

Religion

AD 30 Probable date of the crucifixion of Jesus of Nazareth

Religion

AD 845 Persecution of Buddhists in China is rife

Religion

1170 Archbishop Thomas á Becket is murdered in Canterbury Cathedral

Daily Life

AD 300 Maya of Central America invent a calender

Daily Life

AD 942 Weaving of linen and wool is established in Flanders (Belgium)

Daily Life

1347–1351 The Black Death (bubonic plague) kills 75 million Europeans

Politics	**Politics**	**Politics**
1571 Christian fleet defeats a Turkish fleet at the battle of Lepanto	1642 Civil War breaks out in England between King Charles I and Parliament	1775–1783 American War of Independence from Britain
Exploration	**Exploration**	**Exploration**
1492 Christopher Columbus explores the Americas	1620 Pilgrim Fathers sail to America in the *Mayflower*	1768–1771 James Cook of Britain makes his first round the world voyage
Technology	**Technology**	**Technology**
c.1440 Johannes Gutenberg of Germany begins printing with type	1608 Hans Lippershey of the Netherlands invents the microscope	1709 Abraham Darby of England begins using coke to smelt iron
Arts	**Arts**	**Arts**
1545 First ever book fair is held in Leipzig, Germany	1623 The First Folio prints most of Shakespeare's plays	1735 Imperial ballet school in St. Petersburg, Russia, opens
Religion	**Religion**	**Religion**
1534 English Church breaks from Rome with the monarch as its head	1692 Salem Witch Trials, Massachusetts	1730 John and Charles Wesley establish the Methodist movement
Daily Life	**Daily Life**	**Daily Life**
1565 The first potatoes arrive in Spain from America	1666 The Great Fire destroys most of London	1752 Britain adopts the Gregorian calendar, dropping 11 days

Politics
1804 Napoleon becomes Emperor of France and is finally defeated in 1815

Politics
1861–65 American Civil War: 11 states secede from the Union

Politics
1911 China becomes a republic 1914–18 World War I

Exploration
1803–1806 Lewis and Clark find a route across N. America to the Pacific

Exploration
1872 HMS Challenger begins a world survey of the oceans

Exploration
1911 Roald Amundsen of Norway leads first party to the South Pole

Technology
1814 George Stephenson builds first successful steam locomotive

Technology
1885 Karl Benz of Germany builds the first motor-car

Technology
1903 In the USA, first powered flight of the Wright Brothers

Arts
1827 Joseph Niépce of France takes the world's first photograph

Arts
1874 Impressionist movement in painting starts in Paris

Arts
1905 First regular cinema opens in Pittsburgh, USA

Religion
1808 Napoleon abolishes the Inquisition in Italy and Spain

Religion
1871 Charles Russell founds the Jehovah's Witnesses

Religion
1917 Balfour Declaration: Britain backs homeland for Jews in Palestine

Daily Life
1840 Penny postage and adhesive stamps are introduced

Daily Life
1864 Louis Pasteur of France invents pasteurization

Daily Life
1918 British women over the age of 30 gain the right to vote

Politics
1939–45 World War II involves most of the world's great powers

Politics
1963 US President John F. Kennedy assassinated
1965–73 The Vietnam war

Politics
1991 Collapse of the Soviet Union: republics become independent

Exploration
1932 Auguste Piccard ascends 28 km in a stratospheric balloon

Exploration
1969 Neil Armstrong of the USA is the first person to walk on the Moon

Exploration
1997 US robot explores surface of Mars

Technology
1937 Frank Whittle builds the first jet aero engine

Technology
1967 Christiaan Barnard performs first human heart transplant

Technology
1990s Internet links millions of computers for the first time

Arts
1937 First full-length cartoon film, Snow White and the Seven Dwarfs

Arts
1950s Rock and Roll develops

Arts
1985 Live Aid rock concert raises $60 million for African famine relief

Religion
1948 The World Council of Churches is established

Religion
1968 In Northern Ireland, Catholics and Protestants clash over civil rights

Religion
1978 Election of Pope John II, a Pole and the first non-Italian pope for 456 years

Daily Life
1929 Wall Street crash: world's biggest economic crisis begins

Daily Life
1953 Mount Everest is climbed for the first time

Daily Life
1997 Hong Kong is returned to China

INDEX

127

ACKNOWLEDGEMENTS

The publishers wish to thank the following artists who have
contributed to this book:

Martin Camm, Richard Hook, Rob Jakeway, John James, Shane
Marsh, Roger Payne, Mark Peppé, Eric Rowe, Peter Sarson, Roger
Smith, Michael Welply and Michael White.

The publishers wish to thank the following for supplying photographs
for this book:

Page 6 (BL) Bridgeman Art Library; 23 (TR) ET Archive; 25 (CR)
AKG London; 28 (CR) AKG London; 36 (TL) ET Archive; 43 (TR)
ET Archive; 47 (CR) AKG London; 49 (BL) ET Archive; 52 (CR)
ET Archive; 58 (CR) ET Archive; 61 (TR) AKG London; 63 (TR)
Gerald Kelly Archives; 64-65 (B) ET Archive; 66 (B) AKG London;
67 (BC) AKG London; 79 (TL) ET Archive; 80 (B) AKG London;
85 (T) AKG London; 113 (T) Panos Pictures; 114 (BL) ET Archive;
116 (CR) Rex Features.

All other photographs from Miles Kelly Archives.